Praise for *The Space Within*:

'With rare depth, Michael Neill offers brilliant insights into the mind-boggling upside of being human.'

MIKE DOOLEY, *NEW YORK TIMES* BEST-SELLING AUTHOR OF *INFINITE POSSIBILITIES* AND *LEVERAGING THE UNIVERSE*

'The Space Within *imparts wisdom with warmth and an understanding of what it means to be human in all its shades. A truly enlightening book that will leave you uplifted and comforted in the knowledge that peace does indeed come from within, once we know where to look!'*

ANDY FOWLER, EMMY AWARD-WINNING VISUAL-EFFECTS PRODUCER/PRODUCTION EXECUTIVE ON *THE REVENANT, NOAH,* AND *300*

'At my best as a writer/director, I'm reaching into a space where time stands still and creative ideas flow through like a river. In The Space Within, *Michael Neill offers easy access to this space where creativity comes from, demystifying it without taking away any of its magic.'*

SACHA GERVASI, EMMY AWARD-WINNING DIRECTOR OF *ANVIL! THE STORY OF ANVIL* AND WRITER OF *THE TERMINAL*

'This is an absolutely brilliant book about one of the most important subjects of all: the nothing at the heart of everything. It's the first book I know of that explores in practical, useful detail the space within – the vast context of pure consciousness in which our experience occurs. Reading the book is an evolutionary journey in itself, and I urge you to take up that adventure at your earliest opportunity.'

GAY HENDRICKS, PH.D., AUTHOR (WITH KATHLYN HENDRICKS, PH.D.) OF *CONSCIOUS LOVING EVER AFTER*

'The Space Within *is an invitation to live an impossibly wonderful life. It will help you to move beyond your theories and beliefs about how much happiness is possible and how much is "too good to be true." It will help you to return to love, and to come home to your own innate wisdom.'*

ROBERT HOLDEN, PH.D., BEST-SELLING AUTHOR OF *SHIFT HAPPENS!* AND *LIFE LOVES YOU* (WITH LOUISE HAY)

'Michael Neill has done it again, sharing the secrets of the universe with eloquence and unbridled simplicity. Get it. Read it. Reach for it whenever you need a reminder...'
SHAMA HYDER, AUTHOR OF *MOMENTUM* AND CEO OF ZEN MARKETING

'This is a brilliant book on how to access the space of meditation without meditating. Read, enjoy, and unleash your deepest potential!'
PAUL MCKENNA, PH.D., INTERNATIONAL BEST-SELLING AUTHOR OF *THE THREE THINGS THAT WILL CHANGE YOUR DESTINY TODAY!*

'In this amazing book, Michael Neill lovingly guides us home to the space within. With humor, grace, and simplicity, he invites us to wake up and remember that who we are is infinite.'
ANITA MOORJANI, *NEW YORK TIMES* BEST-SELLING AUTHOR OF *DYING TO BE ME*

'The Space Within contains everything you need to know to be resilient in life broken down in a way that makes it both simple and profound.'
GEORGE PRANSKY, PH.D., AUTHOR OF *THE RELATIONSHIP HANDBOOK*

'Michael has a wonderful way of describing both our spiritual nature and our human nature. He leads the reader to consider both worlds, offering us the opportunity to see the two are One.'
ELSIE SPITTLE, FOUNDER OF 3PHD AND AUTHOR OF *NUGGETS OF WISDOM* AND *BEYOND IMAGINATION*

'As I finished the last page of this powerful book, I wiped tears of gratitude from my cheeks. Not often am I reminded of the true beauty underlining the human condition – beneath the ups and downs and everything in between. Michael Neill points us away from the relentless desire for 24/7 happiness toward the infinite potential life has on offer, not only opening the door but offering up a pillow and a blanket to welcome us home to our deepest self.'
BROOKE WHEELDON-REECE, CEO OF THE CYPRESS INITIATIVE AND CREATOR OF THE S.P.A.R.K. TEEN MENTORING CURRICULUM: SPEAKING TO THE PROMISE, ABILITY, AND RESILIENCE INSIDE KIDS

the
space
[within]

the
space
[within]

FINDING YOUR WAY BACK HOME

MICHAEL NEILL

HAY HOUSE

Carlsbad, California • New York City • London • Sydney
Johannesburg • Vancouver • Hong Kong • New Delhi

First published and distributed in the United Kingdom by:
Hay House UK Ltd, Astley House, 33 Notting Hill Gate, London W11 3JQ
Tel: +44 (0)20 3675 2450; Fax: +44 (0)20 3675 2451; www.hayhouse.co.uk

Published and distributed in the United States of America by:
Hay House Inc., PO Box 5100, Carlsbad, CA 92018-5100
Tel: (1) 760 431 7695 or (800) 654 5126
Fax: (1) 760 431 6948 or (800) 650 5115; www.hayhouse.com

Published and distributed in Australia by:
Hay House Australia Ltd, 18/36 Ralph St, Alexandria NSW 2015
Tel: (61) 2 9669 4299; Fax: (61) 2 9669 4144; www.hayhouse.com.au

Published and distributed in the Republic of South Africa by:
Hay House SA (Pty) Ltd, PO Box 990, Witkoppen 2068
info@hayhouse.co.za; www.hayhouse.co.za

Published and distributed in India by:
Hay House Publishers India, Muskaan Complex, Plot No.3, B-2,
Vasant Kunj, New Delhi 110 070
Tel: (91) 11 4176 1620; Fax: (91) 11 4176 1630; www.hayhouse.co.in

Distributed in Canada by:
Raincoast Books, 2440 Viking Way, Richmond, B.C. V6V 1N2
Tel: (1) 604 448 7100; Fax: (1) 604 270 7161; www.raincoast.com

Text © Michael Neill, 2016

A catalogue record for this book is available from the British Library.

ISBN: 978-1-78180-648-7

Interior images: pp.15–19, 41, 97–98, 118, 120, 126 © David Beeler; p.37 'My wife and my mother-in-law', created by W. E. Hill, 1915; pp.55–56, 58 © Michael Neill

Printed and bound by CPI Group (UK) Ltd, Croydon, CR0 4YY

To Syd Banks and all those who point the way back home

We shall not cease from exploration
And the end of all our exploring
Will be to arrive where we started
And know the place for the first time.

T.S. Eliot, *Four Quartets*

CONTENTS

FOREWORD

The original plan was for four of us to go out to dinner in Kensington, London. However, two friends cancelled at the last minute. Now it was just Michael Neill and me. We barely knew each other. I remember thinking to myself, *I'm sure this will be great, but I'd like to get home by 9:30 p.m.* I don't remember the name of the restaurant. I forget what we ate. The wine was very good, but I can't recall its name. What I do remember is that the conversation was exhilarating, that we left the restaurant at closing time, and that Michael had to pay because it turned out I had forgotten my wallet.

As I sat in the back of the old black cab that was taking me home through Notting Hill to Chiswick, I remember feeling very happy and grateful that I'd met Michael. I felt I'd made a real friend. Suddenly, a thought popped into my mind. It wasn't one of 'my' thoughts. I didn't deliberately think it. It was one of 'those' thoughts that come from nowhere. It was: *Michael will be a lifelong friend and our friendship a great blessing.*

I'm happy to say that Michael and I have been in each other's lives ever since. In the last 10 years or so, we've shared the stage at seminars, supported each other's book launches, appeared as guests on our radio shows, and collaborated on projects like Michael's Supercoach Academy. We've hung out with each other's families, played golf, and wined and dined all over the place, including that night at Bern's Steak House in Tampa when we spent our speaker's fees on a bottle of 1937 Château Cos d'Estournel.

Sydney Banks, discoverer of the Three Principles, said, 'Sometimes one genuine insight is worth all your previous experiences in life.' Over the years, Michael has given me a bucketful of insights. In fact, he collects life-changing insights for fun. He's like the person who finds beautiful shells on the beach just where you were looking a moment ago.

Perhaps best of all, Michael has made me think. He has made me think about thinking and about the nature of mind. Through our conversations, I have learned to cultivate a relationship with my thoughts that has transformed how I experience life.

A central principle of my own work is: *most people don't need more therapy; they need more clarity.* Michael actively demonstrates this in the way that he writes – as a friend who doesn't try to fix you because he knows that you're not really broken. Yes, you might have had a terrible past. Yes, your father may have failed his emotional intelligence exam. Yes, your body may be in terrible pain. Yes, your finances may be a mess. You may be suffering from psychology, and frightening yourself with horrible thoughts.

But if you could see clearly, you'd see that the essence of who you are is untouched by what has happened to you. You would know that you are still okay. What is commonly called a *dark night of the soul* is really *a dark night of the ego*. Knowing this helps you to tap into the space within where healing is possible and miracles happen.

In this book, Michael introduces us to this space within and teaches us how to befriend our mind. He reminds us that we are not our thoughts. We learn how to stop being a victim of our own thinking. We learn to download wisdom, and to think thoughts we've not let ourselves think before.

He teaches that the intellect is only one facet of the mind, and that beyond it is a universal intelligence which is freely available to each of us. If we're willing to put down the book entitled *My Mind*, we can wander around the whole library and even access the thoughts of God.

The Space Within is an invitation to live an impossibly wonderful life. It will help you to move beyond your theories and beliefs about how much happiness is possible and how much is 'too good to be true.' It will help you to return to love, and to come home to your own innate wisdom.

I encourage you to meander your way through these pages. Be leisurely. Read between the lines. Take in the white space behind the words. You are about to meet your original mind. Be ready to be inspired. Make way for miracles.

Robert Holden, Ph.D.
Author of *Shift Happens!* and *Loveability*
London, February 2016

[Introduction]

ONE PROBLEM, ONE SOLUTION

FINDING YOUR TRUE NATURE IS THE KEY TO PRETTY MUCH EVERYTHING.

BE HAPPY AND FOLLOW YOUR PATH

'You see, where we're searching for is our home grounds – we're searching to find the way home. And to find the way home, what you have to do is look at everything in reverse. Because naturally, if you're away from home, if you keep walking, you walk further away. To find home you've got to turn round, and instead of searching outside for the answer you seek, all you do is look inside ... and there lie the secrets that you want.'

Syd Banks

When I was 32 years old, I discovered the secret to life. I dropped into a space inside myself that was so deep and beautiful and clear that everything seemed possible and nothing in my world seemed like a problem. For a period of about six weeks, if there was anything to be done, I just did it; if there was nothing to be done, I didn't waste a single thought thinking about it.

I experienced a depth and purity of peace of mind unlike anything I'd ever known in my life, which carried on for longer than I'd ever imagined possible. The only problem was I had no idea what was happening to me and no idea how to sustain it or get it back if it ever left me.

My first attempt at articulating this secret was simply this:

Be happy.

As no one seemed to find this as profound as it felt to me, my second attempt clarified how to apply the secret:

Be happy
and
follow your path.

While this was an accurate description of how I was living my life during this period, it didn't really seem to work for anybody else, as they all had questions about 'How do I do that?' which I couldn't really answer. The more words I tried to put around what I was experiencing, the less I experienced it, until one day I dropped back into that 'space within' and realized I hadn't touched it for nearly 18 months.

My search for answers about what was happening to me and how I could make it happen again and last for longer continued obsessively for the next seven years. In addition to my already extensive training and experience with neuro-linguistic programming (NLP), a methodology designed to help people hack their own brain, I studied a number of psychological and spiritual disciplines in hopes of being able to reverse engineer my experience. I wanted to not only regain this extraordinary state of mind, but to learn to share it with others.

Then in 2007, much to my own surprise, I found the answer. It lay not in a particular system, philosophy, psychology, religion, practice, or discipline, but in an understanding of our spiritual nature first articulated by an enlightened Scottish welder named Sydney Banks.

Syd, as his biography made very clear, had a basic education and little interest in the human experience other than the universal one of trying to make his life a bit better and his marriage a bit more tolerable. But after a couple of seemingly unrelated events – a glimpse of something in a book by J. Krishnamurti and an offhand comment by a psychologist, who told him, 'You're not *really* insecure, Syd – you just think you are' – he had a spontaneous enlightenment experience.

In his own words:

> I turned around, looked out the picture window at the ocean, and it was like being sucked down a tunnel. All of a sudden, I was buzzing and there was white light all around me, just buzzing, buzzing, and I was in the middle of this light. Nobody

*could see it. Just me. And it was like I was captured in this
white light, and it was just buzz, buzz, buzz. Right there and
then, I realized the true meaning of God. I started to cry.*

*I turned around to [my wife] Barb, and I said, 'I'm home.
I'm free. I've made it. I've conquered this world. This means
to say that you and I will be traveling all over the world.
We're going to change psychology and psychiatry so millions
of people will be healed.*

The experience changed him so fundamentally that his own
colleagues at the pulp mill where he had worked for over a
dozen years didn't recognize him, and his life transformed
much as he had predicted. For the next 36 years he traveled
around the world speaking to tens of thousands of people
from all walks of life. Multiple psychologies formed around
his work – Neo-Cognitive Psychology, Psychology of Mind,
Health Realization – but several attempts to organize a religion
or cult of personality were nipped in the bud when Syd sent
everyone home with the admonition: 'Go live your life.'

While my own experience felt like bumping up against
the tip of the iceberg that had shattered Syd's world into a
million pieces and exposed something beautiful inside, his
experience also seemed familiar to me. One minute, things
looked and felt one way; the next, for no obvious or apparent
reason, they looked and felt 1,000 times more beautiful.
Nothing had changed, but everything was different. I'd

woken up to an awareness of a deeper dimension of life – my spiritual home – and with that awakening a whole new way of being in the world began to emerge.

WHY ME?

Since I'll be taking on the role of 'taxi driver to the deeper dimension' during our time together, let me establish my credentials:

♦ I am not enlightened, nor do I think I am particularly likely to become so during this lifetime.

♦ I eat meat, drink coffee, procrastinate, and get pissed off when people talk or check their phones in the middle of a movie.

♦ I am as f@#ked up, insecure, neurotic, and emotional (i.e., 'FINE') as the next person; however, it has surprisingly little impact on my enjoyment of life or effectiveness in the world.

♦ I am genuinely happy and have been for years – no mean feat for a depressed, suicidal teenager 30 years further on in life.

♦ As a transformative author, coach, speaker, and radio-show host, I have shared this understanding with well over 100,000 people over the past nine years, and the stories they tell me about the changes that have occurred as they've begun to 'get the joke' and find their way back to a deeper part of themselves never cease to amaze me.

If these credentials don't 'wow' you, not to worry – I'm simply trying to point out that a) yes, I'm still human and b) being human can be absolutely amazing as you get further out of your own way and allow the deeper intelligence and energy behind life to fill you up and move you forward.

Here are some of the things people report as the natural effects of waking up to a deeper understanding of the spiritual principles I'll be sharing with you in this book:

♦ a completely new relationship with stress, fear, anger, and every other emotional reaction that can cripple us physically, slow us down mentally, and lead to the disconnection, decay, and even dissolution of our most important relationships with others

♦ higher levels of performance, more time spent in flow states (i.e., 'in the zone'), and access to fresh new thinking and creativity 'on demand'

♦ a deeper experience of connection with life and hope for the future that heals past grievances, leads to natural forgiveness, saves marriages and families, and allows for personal healing of even the worst traumas

♦ an awakening and/or deepening of the spiritual part of ourselves, whether secular or religious in expression

HOW TO GET THE MOST OUT OF OUR TIME TOGETHER

Most books that purport to help you get more out of life fit into one of two categories: informative guides or practical manuals. This book is designed to sit in a third category: as a catalyst to wake you up to something that is already inside you. There's a sense in which you already know everything we'll be talking about, even if you've never consciously thought about it or attempted to put it into words.

For example, after listening to my TEDx talk, 'Why Aren't We Awesomer?', Bob Hurley, the surfer turned CEO of Hurley International, which is now a division of Nike and one of the most profitable lines of sports apparel in the world, took me aside and said, 'That was great, Michael – but can I ask you a question?' When I assured him that he could, he said, somewhat conspiratorially, 'Isn't this all kind of obvious?'

I agreed with him that it was, but also pointed out that, like the naked leader in *The Emperor's New Clothes*, for something that everyone recognized once they saw it, it was remarkable how few people actually saw it in the first place.

Which begs the question of how best to see the elusive obvious. While there's no one right answer, there is definitely a direction in which to look, and it's inside you. Not inside your body, but inside the quiet and spaciousness of your own mind.

Think of 'quiet' not as an absence of thought but as the space inside which the noise of your thinking arises. What makes this tricky, at least to begin with, is that at first glimpse the noise is more interesting than the quiet.

For example, look at the white background of this page. Chances are you can still see the words, and even read them, but without noticing it, at some point you will once again become absorbed in the words and stop seeing the white of the page.

In the same way, it's easy to get caught up in reading and either agreeing or arguing with the words that I'm using and totally miss the space to which they're pointing.

That's not your fault, and in fairness, it's not really my fault either. Trying to explain spiritual truth is like pointing to fire with ice – the closer you get to the reality of what you're pointing to, the less useful your words become.

As Lao Tzu wrote over 5,000 years ago in the *Tao Te Ching*:

> *The Tao which can be expressed in words is not the eternal Tao; the name which can be uttered is not its eternal name.*
>
> *Without a name, it is the Beginning of Heaven and Earth; with a name, it is the Mother of all things.*
>
> *Only one who is eternally free from earthly passions can apprehend its spiritual essence; he who is ever clogged by passions can see no more than its outer form.*

These two things, the spiritual and the material, though we call them by different names, in their origin are one and the same.

This sameness is a mystery – the mystery of mysteries.

It is the gate of all spirituality.

Or as Syd Banks put it a bit more succinctly back in the days of cassette tapes:

If you're driving in your car listening to this and you find yourself in a beautiful feeling, pop the tape out, throw it out the window, and stay with the feeling. The feeling has information in it – it will teach you everything you need to know about life.

In order to make it easier to go beyond the words and find your way back home, you'll find lots of drawings and metaphors throughout this book. They're not designed to be interpreted literally – just enjoy them for what they are, and if one of them doesn't make sense, you can move on to the next.

Each metaphor is prefaced by a reminder that I got from my daughter Maisy's favorite T-shirt:

Something like this but not this.

While for her I think it's meant to be an expression of teenage angst, to me it speaks to the challenge of putting words to the music of life.

Fortunately, the premise of this book is simple:

> There is a space within you where you are already perfect, whole, and complete. It is a space of pure Consciousness – the space inside which all thoughts come and go.
>
> When you rest in the feeling of this space, the warmth of it heals your mind and body. When you operate from the infinite creative potential of this space, you produce high levels of performance and creative flow. When you sit in the openness of this space with others, you experience a level of connection and intimacy which is breathtakingly enjoyable and filled with love. And when you explore this space more deeply, you find yourself growing closer and closer to the divine, even if you're not sure there is such a thing and wouldn't know how to talk about it if there were.
>
> Every problem we have in life is the result of losing our bearings and getting caught up in the content of our own thinking; the solution to every one of those problems is to find our way back home.

One problem. One solution. Infinite possibilities...

[Chapter 1]

HOW TO BE MORE OF WHO YOU REALLY ARE

YOU ARE NOT WHO YOU THINK
YOU ARE – YOU ARE THE SPACE
WHERE THOUGHTS ARISE.

THE STORY OF 'ME'

*'Why are you unhappy? Because 99.9 percent
of everything you think, and of everything you
do, is for yourself – and there isn't one.'*

Wei Wu Wei

In the beginning, there was a field of infinite possibility and pure
potential called the Universal Mind:

Then, somewhere in the midst of the Universal Mind, the thought of you appeared:

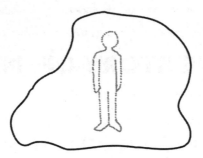

That thought of you became conscious of itself and called itself 'Me.'

For many years, Me lived and played happily in the midst of the garden of everything. But over time, it began to separate and individuate. It went to school and grew up to be an independent, free-thinking, empowered human being, making its way in the world, navigating by the rulebook it had accumulated along the way and using discipline and willpower as its primary engine.

Me grew very strong and enjoyed flexing its muscles and developing its 'personal power.' It forgot all about the Universal Mind that had once been its constant companion:

Eventually, Me began to struggle, as all of us do. It was lonely, and felt insecure, and did everything in its power to make sure that no one ever saw through its façade. It wasn't having a bad life, at least not some of the time, but something was missing.

Then one day, Me heard about something called 'the infinite.' It sounded very important and very grand, and the descriptions of the great peace that could be felt when one touched the infinite sounded like the most beautiful thing Me had ever heard.

But Me was too smart to fall for that one again. After all, the writers of the rulebook inside Me's head had already told it all about a supernatural being who lived in the sky. Since many of the things Me had been told after being born had turned out to be untrue, Me turned its back on its image of the infinite and carried on on its own, struggling more and more but proud of its autonomy and ability to think for itself.

Until one day...

Me met the infinite.

It looked nothing like the image Me had made up in its head, yet it seemed strangely familiar:

Much to Me's surprise, the more time it spent with the infinite, the better life got. In fact, hanging out in the infinite felt like going home to a place Me didn't even remember. Soon, Me and the infinite were spending nearly all of their time together:

Eventually, Me began to think of itself less and less as 'Me' and more and more as a drop in the infinite ocean:

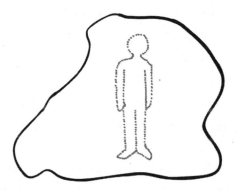

Then one day, Me disappeared. Some said that Me had died, others that Me had become enlightened. But the infinite potential of the Universal Mind remained, and continues on to this day...

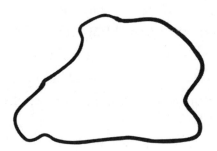

ONE TRUTH, TWO QUESTIONS, THREE PRINCIPLES

In my work as a transformative coach, I've noticed that regardless of whether a client has come to solve a problem, reach a goal, improve a relationship, or unleash their potential, what they really want is the experience of coming alive. It's as if at some level they know they're asleep to the deeper dimensions of life, and they want to wake up and live from a more connected place inside themselves.

So there are really only two questions I'm asking in the back of my mind that are guiding me as to what direction to take in our work together...

1. Do They Know Where Their Experience Is Coming From?

When Syd Banks had his enlightenment experience, he saw that all his insecurities and problems were made of thought and had little or nothing to do with the circumstances of his life. It's not that there isn't a world 'out there,' but that our experience of it is 100 percent an experience of our own thinking.

This is why I often call this work 'the inside-out under-standing.' Until someone begins to recognize that thought is the source of experience (as opposed to genetics, environment, personal history, or any other external circumstance), they have no choice but to focus their energies on fixing, changing, or otherwise altering those external factors in an attempt to enhance and improve their experience of life.

Once they recognize thought as the missing link between the infinite creative potential of the mind and the individual experience of life that they are having, the compulsion to do something to improve their plight diminishes. This not only leaves them in a fairly consistent state of wellbeing regardless of circumstance, it also opens them up to fresh new thinking that makes effecting changes in the world significantly easier.

From this space of wellbeing, a second question begins to emerge:

2. Do They Know That They're God?

One of my colleagues in the inside-out understanding, Mark Howard, told me a story about how he first learned to go deeper into the space within with his clients. Early in his career, he developed a reputation for helping people addicted to drugs and alcohol and was proud of the work he was doing. He was boasting a bit to one of his teachers when to his surprise the teacher said to him: 'It's wonderful that you're helping these people overcome their addictions, but do you know that they're God?'

That one question really hit home, and he realized that he was settling for a very small change in his clients relative to what was possible. He could see that once they knew that they were God, they would begin to realize the limitless potential of their true nature.

I still get uncomfortable from time to time when I share stories like this, as my own habitual thinking about God, religion, and spirit gets all muddled up and I struggle to separate the baby from the bathwater.

But when I say 'God,' I'm not talking religion. I'm simply pointing as best I can to the impersonal energy and intelligence behind life that causes grass to grow, cuts to heal, rain to fall, and inspiration to strike. It's the invisible but pervasive energy of spirit that, in the words of the physicist David Bohm, 'infuses all living things' and is 'that which is truly alive in living systems.' We are of that invisible life energy in the same way that a wave is of the ocean or a cloud is of the sky.

When people think they are nothing more than a body and brain, they feel left to their own devices, only able to achieve as much as their physical limitations and the realities of their environment and upbringing will allow. But when they become aware of a deeper intelligence behind their thinking as an ever-present source of both wisdom and fresh possibility, a wider world opens up to them.

Most of us recognize that at times we are able to access a wisdom which seems to come from somewhere beyond our personal databank and contains information and ideas outside our current knowledge. This wisdom and the insights that come from it sometimes gain an almost mythical status in our thinking, and a lot of superstition often crops up around their appearance.

Yet when we come to see that we can have fresh new thinking at any moment, wisdom stops looking like a big deal or a mystical process and appears to us as a function of the natural resource of a deeper Mind – the ever-present spiritual energy behind life.

As we learn more about the nature of this 'Universal Mind' and begin to glimpse more of its infinite creative potential, we come to rely on it more and more in a variety of situations. We allow ourselves to become reflective and receptive to this wisdom that seems to exist somewhere beyond the reach of our own experience. And in so doing, we tap into the unknown as the very source of both inspiration and creation.

'Mind' is just one of the three fundamental principles that Syd identified as being at the heart of the human experience. When we talk about principles, we're talking about things in their most elemental form – that irreducible level at which things have been made as simple as possible but not simpler.

Here's how Syd articulated 'the three principles' in his book *The Missing Link*:

The Universal Mind, *or the* impersonal mind, *is constant and unchangeable. The personal mind is in a perpetual state of change. All humans have the inner ability to synchronize their personal mind with their impersonal mind to bring harmony into their lives…*

Consciousness is *the gift of awareness. Consciousness allows the recognition of form, form being the expression of* Thought… *Mental health lies within the consciousness of all human beings, but it is shrouded and held prisoner by our own erroneous thoughts. This is why we must look past our contaminated thoughts to find the purity and wisdom that lie inside our own consciousness…*

Thought is *the creative agent we use to direct [ourselves] through life. Thought is the master key that opens the world of reality to all living creatures… Thought is not reality; yet it is through Thought that our realities are created.*

So what does this all mean? It means that there is an extraordinary creative potential which lies largely dormant inside human beings (Mind), that we have the capacity to experience that potential when we look past the illusion of our own thinking (Consciousness), and that there is a creative force (Thought) which serves as a vehicle for creating our personal reality.

But if Mind, Consciousness, and Thought are what makes up our reality, there's another question remaining: who are we?

A CASE OF MISTAKEN IDENTITY

Imagine that Bill Gates comes to you for business coaching. At first you're puzzled, because it would seem that Bill Gates doesn't really need business coaching, but then you realize that he has amnesia and has no idea who he is.

Here's the question:

> *Do you use your sessions to try to give him business advice, or do you spend your time together doing everything you can to help him remember who he really is and what he's really got going for him?*

While it may (or may not) take a bit longer to work toward him remembering his true identity than to offer your personal insights into how best to handle the latest crisis (or opportunity) at Microsoft, the difference in outcome is liable to be phenomenal.

But what if you're the one with amnesia? Are you who you think you are? Is your body merely an icon in the game of life with a name and a backstory that tells you how well or poorly your character is meant to play the game?

To view the question of who you really are in a different light, consider the question of 'the University' as laid out by British philosopher Gilbert Ryle in his book *The Concept of Mind*:

> *A foreigner visiting Oxford or Cambridge for the first time is shown a number of colleges, libraries, playing fields, museums, scientific departments and administrative offices.*
>
> *He then asks, 'But where is the University? I have seen where the members of the Colleges live, where the Registrar works, where the scientists experiment and the rest. But I have not yet seen the University in which reside and work the members of your University.'*

So where is the University really?

Is it in:

A. The buildings and grounds?

B. The students and professors?

C. The interplay between them?

D. The spirit of education that infuses them all with 'University-like' qualities?

E. All (or none) of the above?

Substitute 'the self' for 'the University' and we have the paradox at the heart of all attempts at self-improvement: where is the separate 'self' that we are trying to improve?

Is it in:

A. Our mind and body?

B. Our thoughts and emotions?

C. Our behavior?

D. The spirit that animates us – what Ryle called 'the ghost in the machine'?

E. All (or none) of the above?

It seems to me that there is no one 'thing' that can be pointed to as 'the University,' even though we can identify its many parts; similarly, there is no one 'separate self' to be improved.

In the midst of my early attempts at spiritual spelunking, I read in numerous texts that 'the self' was like an onion. As an experiment, I bought an actual onion from my local greengrocer, took it to Hyde Park, and tried to peel away the layers to see what lay at its core.

To my initial disappointment, there *was* no core – even the smallest part of the center could be peeled away as just another skin. This is the nihilistic view of the self – that because there is nothing but emptiness at our core, there is no meaning, purpose, or value to our life.

But a few moments later I had a *kenshō* experience – a momentary glimpse of the vastness of our true nature. For the nothingness at the core of the onion that had seemed so empty a moment before was suddenly filled with *everything* – the entire park, the city of London, and the universe beyond. From nothing came everything; from emptiness came a fullness of feeling that I can remember to this day.

And this is the good news about our true nature. Just as we don't need to find the 'real' University in order to benefit from its apparent existence, we don't need to pump up the separate self in order to live a full and rich and meaningful life. We are nothing, but we are also everything – and in that paradox lies the secret to pretty much everything…

Imagine for a moment that you are a drop of water. As it happens, you are a very unique little drop – beautifully shaped, with only a cute little distortion in the way you reflect the light. People praise your beauty, and in time you come to believe that you are special.

But as time goes on, you become lonely. You long for the companionship of an other – another drop of water who will love you as you love it and help you feel less alone. You find that other, or you don't; you fall in love, or you don't.

And then one day it starts to rain. Seven billion drops of rain fall in a single afternoon and you are no longer alone. Briefly, you touch mitochondria with a single raindrop and before you know it, two have become one. You are still alone, but you are larger than before. With each drop of water you merge with, your entire being expands, until all seven billion drops become one ocean.

And you are still alone. And all is well.

FINDING YOUR WAY BACK HOME

In his classic book *The Road Less Traveled*, author M. Scott Peck shares the following analogy:

> If one wants to climb mountains one must have a good base camp, a place where there are shelters and provisions, where one may receive nurture and rest before one ventures forth again to seek another summit. Successful mountain climbers know that they must spend at least as much time, if not more, in tending to their base camp as we do in climbing mountains, for their survival is dependent upon their seeing to it that their base camp is sturdily constructed and well stocked.

While he was using the analogy in the context of what it takes to have a successful marriage, the same is true for us as individuals – if we want to achieve great things in life, it is necessary to spend at least as much time, if not more, in tending to our base camp as we actually do in climbing mountains.

What is 'base camp' for us?

It is our essential spiritual (i.e., non-physical) nature – our connection to the whole.

There is a deeper part of all of us that remains unchanged regardless of what our body and personality have been through in life. It is the innate wellbeing that we were born into, the innate wisdom that guided us at key moments in our life when we suddenly knew what to do from a place which seemed somehow outside our normal consciousness yet absolutely right and true.

When we are in touch with that place, we have a sense of expansiveness and possibility. The world feels vast, yet we feel up to the challenge of living in it because we too, at this level of understanding, are vast. It is the space where miracles happen – predictable synchronicities which deliver 'unforeseen incidents, meetings and material assistance which no man could have dreamt would come his way.'*

From this place, we feel we can take on the world because, in a very real way, we *are* the world.

So why do we ever lose sight of 'base camp'? Why do we so often feel small, and less than, and not enough? Why is it

---

* W.H. Murray, *The Scottish Himalayan Expedition*, J.M. Dent, 1951, page 7.

that one minute we're up for anything and the next we're good for nothing?

Because we live in a world of unrecognized thought. Thought is the architect of both hope and despair, the source of every color in the emotional rainbow. Without thought, there would be no delineation in our world, like the pure clarity of light before it passes through a prism and bursts into a kaleidoscope of color.

But unrecognized thought demands our attention and fills our consciousness. And when we get caught up in thought, we lose our way.

It's like being disoriented by mist rolling into base camp. Whether the 'mist' of thought takes the form of a beautiful vision or an icy chill, it can blind us to what is already present and make us feel as though we need to go stumbling about in search of instant remedies instead of waiting for the mist to clear.

In fact, you don't even have to wait – you can just close your eyes to the mist, turn away from the noise, and realize that no matter where you are in your life or in the world, you're never more than one thought away from home. Unlike in the mountain-climbing metaphor, you take your base camp with you on every climb. Whether or not you are aware of that fact is the only variable.

You're already home. You always were. It's just that when you're not preoccupied with your own thinking, it's easier to feel it. And when you know that you can climb mountains in the world without ever leaving home base, going out and trying new things becomes a lot less scary and a lot more fun.

[Chapter 2]

THOUGHT IS NOT WHAT YOU THINK

UNDERSTANDING THE NATURE OF THOUGHT FREES US FROM THE ILLUSION OF OUR THINKING.

SUICIDAL IDEATION

*'The World can be compared to ice, and Truth
to the water from which this ice is formed.'*
Abdul Karim Jili

In 1986, I was not a happy kid. I had no external reasons for being unhappy – I was loved, in good health, and had friends. But I was so unhappy that I also had a thing I now know is called 'suicidal ideation,' which meant that I thought about killing myself pretty much all day, every day.

This wasn't as much of a problem as you might think, because I was a full-time university student with a very busy schedule and relatively little time to think. But it was always going on in the background, and when it would get a bit quieter on the outside, it would get a whole lot noisier on the inside.

This all came to a head a few months into the school year, when I had what I now know is called a 'psychotic break from reality.' If you want to get a sense of what that was like, imagine being in my dorm room on the fourth floor and a giant vacuum cleaner appearing in the sky and sucking your heart out of your body and out of the window.

This was actually terrifying to me because it really felt like it was happening. I hung onto the wall of my dorm room for dear life. There was a phone on the floor, and I reached down with one hand and dialed the number for the suicide hotline … and got a busy signal.

Now even then, being sucked out of the window by a giant vacuum cleaner from hell, I found that funny. In fact, I can't imagine what anyone could have said to me that would have done me more good than that busy signal.

Why?

Because it just kind of 'popped' it in my head. Even though the situation hadn't changed, it didn't seem so compelling or real. I was able to reach back down and phone a friend. She came and got me, and eventually I fell asleep.

I woke up the next morning and realized something kind of profound: I didn't want to kill myself. I didn't want to die. In fact, I so didn't want to die that I'd used every ounce of strength I had to stay in that room, even when it felt like I was being forcibly pulled out of the window.

And that was the first time I realized that just because you have a thought in your head, it doesn't mean that it's *your* thought. It doesn't mean it's true, and it doesn't mean that it's actually what you think. It just means *there's a thought in your head*.

The next time the thought about killing myself came to mind, I wasn't scared of it anymore. I realized that I didn't have to do anything about it. It was just a thought.

THE NATURE OF THOUGHT

There's a famous drawing that's often used to highlight the way that our mind will 'make up' a reality based on what it thinks it's seeing:

Now, take a moment to look at the picture. Do you see an old woman with a big nose and a haggard expression, or do you see a young woman with a button nose and fluttering eyelashes?

Is this really a picture of an old woman or a young woman?

Well, both – or neither. But the question points to how we think the mind works. We think the mind is a camera recording what's really going on 'out there.' Depending on how we use the camera, we'll have a different experience of the world.

So if we photograph the woman from one angle, she's really old, but if we photograph her from another angle, she's really young. If we look at life one way, it's kind of depressing, but if we look at it another way, it's kind of wonderful.

And that's the idea behind positive thinking. If we change our attitude – the angle at which we hold the camera of our mind – we get a different experience of life.

But here's the thing: this isn't a picture of an old woman and it isn't a picture of a young woman. It's a series of lines on a piece of paper. We're the ones creating both the old woman and the young woman without any effort whatsoever and without any conscious intention. What allows us to do that is the power of Thought.

Here's another optical illusion, known as 'the Kanizsa triangle':

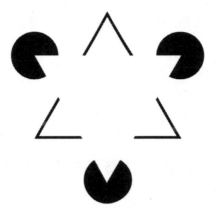

Nearly everyone who looks at this image can clearly see a bold, white upside-down triangle connecting and overlapping an equilateral black triangle and three black dots in the picture. Yet when we look again, we realize that we're not only imagining both triangles, we're also imagining the dots. (Personally, I think they look like little 'Pac-Men,' but I've heard 'fortune cookies' and 'pies with a slice missing' equally often.)

In the same way, when someone 'makes us mad,' it really looks as though they are causing our upset. Yet when our thinking quietens down, the upset tends to disappear. If we look closely, we can see the idea that another person can make us feel a certain way is as illusory as the 'white triangle' we hallucinate when we look at the image above.

And that is why the physicist David Bohm said, 'Thought creates our world and then says, "I didn't do it."'

We live in a world of thought, but we think we live in a world of external experience. The mind is not a camera, it's a projector. We can't tell the difference between an imagined experience 'in here' and what's going on 'out there' – and that confusion creates a lot of confusion.

WHY YOUR THINKING DOESN'T MATTER AS MUCH AS YOU THINK

Remember, a fundamental principle is something that is true, constant, and operational whether you believe it or not. For example, gravity is a fundamental principle of the physical world. As Galileo is said to have demonstrated by dropping two objects of different mass from the Leaning Tower of Pisa, what you believe about gravity makes no difference whatsoever to the rate and speed an object falls if dropped from your hand. And unlike Wile E. Coyote in *The Road Runner* cartoons, the moment we step off a cliff we begin to fall, whether we believe in gravity or not, and even before we notice we are no longer on solid ground.

So the principle of Thought isn't pointing to the content of our thinking, but rather the formless creative energy out of which we construct our personal reality. It is the snow that we make snowmen out of – the play dough of the mind. And in the same way that making shapes is one of the things we can do with play dough, one of the things we can do with Thought is think.

In this sense, Thought is not the stuff that's whizzing around inside our head – those are *thoughts*, fresh out of the oven and already formed. Once a thought is in your head, it's no longer just play dough – it's *made* of play dough. And regardless of whether that thought is positive or negative, an accurate accounting or pure make-believe, Thought itself remains pure creative potential. In other words, no matter how crappy your habitual thinking may be, there's always a fresh batch of play dough ready and waiting to be formed into something new.

What throws us – and it happens again and again and again – is that we think only some of our experience is made of Thought while the rest of our experience is 'real.'

Let's say I worry about my health:

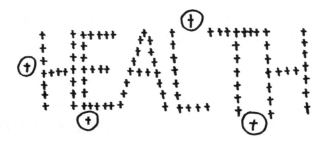

I'm aware that all those little ⊕s are made of thought, and they drive me crazy. They keep me awake at night. So I try to fix that thinking, and be more positive, and stop myself from worrying. Or I try and think less about it, or not to think about it at all. But what gets missed in all of that activity is that the thing itself – my 'health' – is made of Thought too.

> Imagine an iceberg. It doesn't look as though it could possibly be made of the same stuff as the water it's rising out of, but it is. And the sky that surrounds it certainly doesn't look as though it's made up of the same stuff as the iceberg and the water, but fundamentally it is.

When people begin to see that but for their thinking, they would never experience pressure or stress and would consistently experience themselves as perfect and whole, it's not uncommon for them to get annoyed by the fact that they think. They start to think of Thought as the enemy, and, like swatting mosquitos on a hot summer's day, use distraction and/or meditation to gain relief from the universal affliction of 'too much noise in the head.'

But while a quiet mind is certainly a worthy goal, trying to eliminate thinking is a pretty terrible strategy for achieving it. The more we try not to think, the more persistent and powerful our thoughts appear to be. Before long we're booking on the 'advanced meditation program' and/or ordering the family-size glass of wine. The harder we work to get rid of our thinking, the more thinking there is to get rid of. Even if we're successful from time to time, the energy of Thought keeps generating new thinking, and at some point we realize we're fighting a losing battle.

If instead of trying to stop our thinking we sit back, relax, and really reflect on the transient nature of Thought, we begin to see the infinite forms it can take and the constant Mind inside which the game of life plays itself out. Our thinking begins to appear no more (or less) than a series of fluctuations in energy and form, like clouds in the sky, particles in a physics lab, or shadows in a playground. And because we recognize that every shadow is just a side effect of light, we are extremely unlikely to spend much time studying their patterns, reading meaning into their presence or absence, or trying to avoid the 'bad' shadows or create more 'good' ones.

In fact, when our thoughts appear to us as ephemeral as the clouds in the sky, we can appreciate their beauty without worrying about what form they happen to be taking. In the same way that a cloud shaped like a lion is no more dangerous to us than a cloud shaped like a teddy bear, a thought about all the terrible things that might happen has no more power in and of itself than a thought about who's going to win the lottery or how many jelly beans are in the jar at the fair.

Of course, from time to time a particularly horrific-looking cloud might catch our eye and we'll get lost in our fear of the storm we're sure it will unleash. But the moment we remember that we are *not* our thinking, we are the space where thoughts arise, we can experience the storm with the awe of an arctic explorer seeing the aurora borealis, with the delight of a sailor watching the liquid dance of St. Elmo's fire, or with the impartiality of the sky. When the storm has run its course, we'll continue on our way, unaffected by the content of our thinking but deeply touched by the gift of Thought, the Consciousness that allows us to experience it, and the ever-present Mind inside which life continues to unfold.

If this all feels like too much to think about, consider this:

♦ You are already perfect, whole, and mentally healthy exactly as you are.

♦ You are always capable of convincing yourself otherwise.

[Chapter 3]

BECOMING HUMAN

THE GREAT GOAL IS NOT TO ESCAPE
THE HUMAN EXPERIENCE; IT IS TO
EMBRACE AND TRANSCEND IT.

ABANDONING THE PURSUIT OF 24/7 HAPPINESS

*'But if in your fear you would seek only
love's peace and love's pleasure,
Then it is better for you that you cover your
nakedness and pass out of love's threshing-floor,
Into the seasonless world where you
shall laugh, but not all of your laughter,
and weep, but not all of your tears.'*

Kahlil Gibran

When I first began studying psychology and spirituality, I did it for completely selfish reasons. I was emotionally unstable, deeply depressed, and felt victimized by my brain chemistry. Anything that looked as though it would give me the edge against such a fearsome enemy within was something I wanted to know about. Over the ensuing 18 years, I studied multiple disciplines, receiving nine separate certifications in fields ranging from positive psychology to Thought Field Therapy to neuro-linguistic programming. I also experimented with various 'medicines,' from drugs and alcohol to rituals and practices I came to call my 'behavioral Prozac.'

But despite the rich variety of theories, practices, and methodologies, my goal was always the same: to get more control over my emotional experience and move in the direction of 24/7 happiness – a life of only positive feelings without any anger, sadness, insecurity, or fear.

And there's no question that my life got better. I was less unhappy more of the time, and capable of functioning at a much higher level when the black dog of misery had me in its grip.

So when I came across the principles behind the inside-out understanding, I did so in search of yet another weapon for my arsenal in the war against my darker nature. What I found, however, wasn't what I'd gone looking for. Instead of discovering an even better way to manage my moods, I discovered that my emotions weren't reflecting my nature – that they were in fact simply surface fluctuations atop a deep core of wellbeing.

To be honest, this discovery was equal parts liberating and disturbing. Having spent so much of my life battling against my moods (and often even winning the battle), to discover that I was only conquering shadows and defeating imaginary enemies was a bit disillusioning. Fortunately, as I got more deeply in touch with the peace of Mind, disillusionment started to look like a really good idea.

I quickly diagnosed myself with a disease I made up, which I named 'emotophobia':

Emotophobia (n)

[ih-**moh**-t*uh*-**foh**-bee-*uh*]

noun

1. an abnormal or pathological fear of emotions, particularly those thought of as 'negative' or 'non-productive'

Ironically, my first inkling that I suffered from emotophobia was during a mass 'phobia cure' for people with fear of public speaking back when I was still co-leading NLP trainings. As literally hundreds of people took their place on stage to speak to hundreds more in the audience, my colleague was working with one particular man who rated his fear as 10 out of 10. Soon enough, that fear was down to a level 3, but my colleague wasn't satisfied until it was a 1.

Close to an hour later, the man's fear had disappeared and I had had a major insight:

> *I really didn't mind being scared from*
> *time to time when I spoke on stage.*

In fact, I was quite often at a 3 or higher when I was speaking in front of groups and I rarely gave it a second thought. Consequently, it had little or no impact on my ability to perform. In fact, the only time my emotional state seemed to have a direct correlation to my level of performance was in those situations where I thought I needed to feel a certain way in order to successfully complete a particular task.

Once I noticed this, I got less and less worried about my own emotional weather. I started to see that emotophobia was fairly prevalent in our culture, fueling far more of our behavior (and more of the sales of self-help books) than I'd imagined.

You need go no further than your local supermarket to see the fear of 'negative emotions' in action. Wait for the first child to burst into tears and then watch the grown-ups react. Chances are that within a minute you'll see at least one person shake their head in disgust (at child or parent or both), many turn away so they don't get caught up in the drama, and at least one come over to help put the child out of their misery.

Having assisted thousands of people in overcoming phobias and changing the way they feel about different life events, it's not that I don't recognize the fact that we can change our emotional states through techniques and practice.

But if feelings are no more (or less) than the shadows of the thoughts that pass through our mind from moment to moment, why would we?

The simple truth is this:

There's no such thing as a solution to a feeling.

Because we don't recognize this fact, we spend huge chunks of our time and energy trying to 'solve' our feelings by changing them to 'better' ones or eliminating them altogether. Which is kind of like trying to fix the weather, or avoiding people wearing red T-shirts because we don't like the way we feel when we see them.

By way of contrast, there's a story about a psychologist coming up to Syd Banks after a talk and saying, 'Well, that's all very interesting, Syd, but what do we do about anger? Are you suggesting we should just repress it? Won't it be sublimated and come out somewhere else?'

Syd seemed baffled by the question, so one of his friends who was standing nearby came over to help translate.

'I think what he's asking, Syd,' began the friend, 'is what is an appropriate response to the feeling of anger?'

This didn't help, and Syd kindly continued to listen as the two men went back and forth trying to make the question explicit.

Finally, the exasperated psychologist asked, 'Don't you ever get angry, Syd?'

'Of course I do,' Syd responded.

'Well, when you're angry, what do you do about it?'

Syd looked more confused than ever.

'Why would I do anything about it?'

When it's okay to feel good when you feel good and bad when you feel bad, recognizing that as thoughts change, the feelings change with them, there's no need to prefer one feeling over another, let alone attempt to fix it.

And when you really see that for yourself, you begin to experience more of the deeper feelings that make life worth living.

WELCOME TO THE HUMAN CONDITION

Since I first began looking in this direction, I've also come to see that while the human potential is essentially infinite, most people (including me) live in a relatively limited range of that potential. Despite a couple of decades at the cutting edge of the worlds of self-help, positive psychology, and personal development, I can still be mean-spirited, petty, and small-minded. And despite my best efforts (and the best efforts of some of the most successful and highest-paid people in the field), I still get overcome from time to time by a level of fear and insecurity that would be comically irrational if it wasn't me who had to wade through it.

This isn't to say that my life isn't significantly better than it was before I started – I've gone from being a depressed teenager with suicidal ideation to an incredibly happy, loved, and successful 'grown-up.' But I still get visited by some of the insecure thoughts and hang-ups that made my life such a misery when I was younger. The only real difference is that, by and large, I've made my peace with the fact that no matter how 'spiritually enlightened' I might get, I'm always going to have to deal with my very human psychology.

And this points to one of the biggest differences I've seen between the inside-out understanding and traditional psychology. Tell a typical therapist or self-help guru that you're upset about your childhood, argumentative with your partner or children, and struggling with financial insecurity, and they'll quickly reframe your problems in a positive light, affirm your greatness, and offer up seven simple steps to a happier childhood, better marriage, and financial abundance.

Say the same thing to someone who's insightfully seen that we live in the feeling of our thinking, not the feeling of the world, and they'll most likely say, 'Me too – welcome to the human condition.' They'll then point you inside, toward a fresh experience of your deeper nature – the innate wellbeing, peace of mind, and inner wisdom that allow us to navigate our lives with ease and grace in spite of the insecure thinking and bizarrely counter-productive behavior we all engage in from time to time.

So while I would love to be less vain, more humble, and less scared of my own shadow, I also love that I can live a wonderful life even in the occasional company of my vanity, arrogance, and fear.

BEYOND HAPPINESS

If you spend any time around young children (or, if I'm being honest, Hollywood actors and actresses), you'll notice the journey from happy to sad to angry to fearful to loving is on a pretty continual loop.

I call this phenomenon the 'sine curve of emotion,' as the rise and fall of our moods and emotions tends to go up and down with the consistency and predictability of a mathematical equation.

Of course, whereas a traditional sine curve looks something like this:

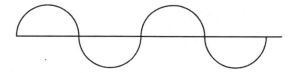

our emotional sine curve looks a bit more like this:

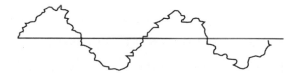

As a culture, we have a tendency to become as obsessive about explaining and tracking these highs and lows as traders and investors are about tracking the stock market. And as with the markets, we continue to hope against hope that if only we can discover a secret magic formula, we'll be able to prop the sine curve up at the top so that we can sustain longer and longer highs and avoid those nasty lows.

There are a couple of different ways we attempt to do this. The first is to try and master the art of positive thinking. Because at some level we recognize that our emotions follow our thoughts, we try to control our thoughts to master our emotions. The problem with this strategy, as we've already seen, is that Thought doesn't seem to lend itself to control over time, and nearly everybody experiences a backlash from this 'fake it 'til you make it' kind of approach.

The resultant artificially altered curve tends to wind up looking something like this:

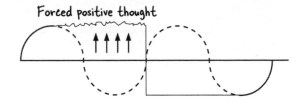

We may be able to maintain a positive emotional state for an extended period of time, but, like an Olympic power-lifter attempting to set a new world record, when our attention flags for even a second, the whole thing comes crashing down to the ground with a bang.

The second way we try to avoid the ups and downs of the emotional sine curve is to completely deaden ourselves to our emotions, attempting to stay at a comfortable 5 on a scale from 1 to 10. For a time, this detached apathy can be a relief from the crazy up and down ride of the sine curve, and we can easily confuse it with peace of mind. The difference is, peace of mind actually feels good, while the apathy of detachment doesn't feel like much of anything.

Fortunately, there's some good news coming – a pot of gold hidden underneath this emotional rainbow. For at all times, independent of circumstances and independent of thoughts and emotion, there is a world of deeper feeling available to us.

While we sometimes give these deeper feelings emotional labels, like 'gratitude,' 'humility,' 'awe,' 'peace,' 'joy,' and 'bliss,' what sets them apart is their unconditionality – their consistent presence through time, regardless of how things are going in our life. They are the constant backdrop against which our emotional life unfolds – the space out of which our thoughts and emotions arise and back into which they dissolve.

For me, it seems this world of deeper feeling is a part of our birthright – the simple feeling of being alive that we were born with, uncontaminated by the wild imaginings of our personal thinking. And the moment my thoughts settle, regardless of where I happen to be on the emotional sine curve, these deeper feelings rise closer and closer to the surface until they break through into my consciousness.

I often think of these deeper feelings in terms of water – a river that flows with peace and wellbeing, a well of being which we can always dip into, or an ocean of consciousness that surrounds me at all times.

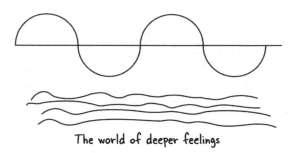

The world of deeper feelings

It's something like this (but not this):

Imagine that you are riding on a giant barge floating gently down a beautiful river. In the very center of the barge is a giant roller coaster, and your seat for the journey is in the front car. As the river carries the barge downstream, the roller coaster goes up and down, pausing every now and again before climbing its way to the next peak or plunging its way down into a valley. At times it spins wildly, completely disorienting you; at other times, you find yourself resting in the pause between rides.

Now imagine that your whole life you have ridden with your eyes closed, believing that the roller coaster is the world and the river only a myth. What would happen the first time you opened your eyes and kept them open for every moment of the ride?

At first, you might be a bit disoriented and even frightened as you watched yourself and others going up and down and around and around at occasionally dizzying speeds. The first time you crested the heights of the coaster and saw the river in all its glory, you would be so taken by the view that you would never want it to end. And when your revelation was followed by a plunge to the bottom, it would seem that all was lost.

But over time, you would begin to relax into the ride, spending less and less time trying to manage the ups and downs and more and more time enjoying the views along the way. You'd take comfort in the fact that no matter what was going on with the roller coaster, the river was always effortlessly supporting the barge along its journey. And you might even begin to enjoy pondering the mysteries of where the river came from, how you came to be on it, and where it might be taking you...

I'd always thought that to transcend something was to move past it – i.e., to leave it in my rear-view mirror as I carried on speeding my way towards enlightenment. Yet what I've realized is that to transcend is not to leave behind but to expand beyond. It's less about floating above the muck of life than being able to go down into it without any fear of drowning in it.

In this sense, waking up to your spiritual nature is like being a Russian nesting doll. Even as you expand into higher levels of consciousness and understanding, you still take the lower levels with you. And instead of using spiritual understanding as an avoidance strategy, we can use it as a safety net, allowing us to experience our human thoughts and emotions evermore deeply, knowing that the intelligence and peace of Mind will always be there to catch us if we fall.

So I can experience my natural ups and downs without so much of the accompanying story and drama. I'm less hypnotized by my highs and frightened by my lows. I can sob without suffering and feel fear without being afraid. My divinity can inform my humanity. My heart can break open without breaking apart.

For me, the unexpected gift of this deeper understanding is that I've never been more willing to feel my frailty – and I've never felt stronger or more whole in my entire life.

Abandoning the pursuit of happiness has revealed a deeper truth and an even more magical possibility: the timeless presence of the space within, a river of wisdom and wellbeing that is no less present when we're down than where we're up, and no less powerful when we feel weak than when we feel on top of the world.

This timeless presence is our true nature – the essential well of our being – and the true source of peace in our life. So while I may still find myself in a crappy mood from time to time, it hardly seems worth thinking about, let alone trying to fix by figuring it out, tapping it away, or medicating it into oblivion. This too will pass, and remembrance of the river is never more than a thought away.

[Chapter 4]

THE PEACE OF MIND

THE PEACE OF MIND IS BOTH
THE PATH AND THE GOAL OF
THE SPIRITUAL JOURNEY.

GOING DEEPER

'The very inquiry into what is meditation
will open the door to meditation...'

J. Krishnamurti

When I first began learning about the Three Principles, I threw myself into the field with my usual 'kitchen sink' abandon, reading every book multiple times, listening to every audio I could get my hands on, going on every course, and peppering practitioners with questions at every opportunity.

Less than a year after recognizing the fact that we live in the feeling of our thinking, not the feeling of our circumstances, I was quieter in my mind than I'd ever been. For the first time in my life, I didn't feel broken. I recognized that the only thing between me and my wellbeing was a thought, and that I didn't even have to control my thinking – I could simply let it settle and my mind would return to a relatively quiet and peaceful place all by itself.

So when one of my teachers suggested that there were deeper levels to this understanding, I was genuinely puzzled. It was such a relief to finally be 'fixed' that I couldn't imagine what could be gained by continuing to look in this direction.

But after taking some time off from all that studying, I became intrigued by the idea that there might be something beyond the levels of wellbeing that I felt I'd already discovered, and I returned to the conversation.

This time, I didn't really know what I was looking for, so I read and watched and listened with less vigor and intention than before. Because I was more relaxed and had less on my mind, I was able to see and hear things that had eluded me the first time around.

To my own surprise, I began to spend more and more of my time in the world of deeper feeling that I've been describing throughout our time together. This meditative place inside me seemed to fit the description of what some Eastern religions call 'the unconditioned mind,' and I began to experience a level of connection and insight that led me to begin describing it as 'the space where miracles happen.'

Better still, the more time I spent in that space, the more my family, friends, and people around me seemed to spend in it too. It was as if the space itself had a resonance that drew people into it like a gravitational field. But when people asked me to explain this 'second order' change, I struggled. I couldn't identify what was different between 'just' getting quieter and this deeper sense of peace, clarity, and wellbeing.

As I've continued to look in this direction over the past number of years, I've become clearer and clearer that the difference that makes the difference in the quality of our life and the level of our effectiveness in the world is less to do with having a quiet mind than with what shows up in that space of quiet.

Or to put it another way:

There is a world of difference between experiencing an absence of thought and the presence of Mind.

When I allow myself to go beyond the relief of a quiet mind and rest in the mystery and presence of a larger divine Mind, it feels like coming home. The world begins to make sense again, my love for and faith in humanity grow, and I get to experience a level of peace in the midst of the chaos that allows me to embrace the richness of life in a way that the younger me who 'just wanted to be happy' could never have imagined.

This peace is, as best as I can tell, our birthright as human beings. And the kindness of the design is that all we ever need to do to claim it is to look in this direction and to see it for ourselves.

In order to better understand what this profound sense of peace really is and where it comes from, let's take a look at four different things that people tend to mean when they use the phrase 'peace of mind.'

1. The Absence of Conflict

As long as no one's upset with me, I will have peace of mind.

At a very basic level, peace of mind looks like the absence of conflict. So if we want to experience more of it, we need to either get better at conflict management or simply avoid conflict altogether.

People who equate peace of mind with an absence of conflict might think of themselves as 'peacemakers,' but as often as not they're really just 'avoiders of conflict.' (Think Neville Chamberlain before World War II or a long-suffering spouse who puts up with all sorts of abusive behavior from their partner in hopes of a quiet life.)

Not only does this overly conciliatory head-in-the-sand attitude tend to create more conflict than it avoids, it also keeps our head filled with boatloads of thought about what we mustn't do or say, which in turn eliminates any chance we might have of actually experiencing peace of mind in the first place.

Which is why at some point most people start to realize that absence of conflict is less important than…

2. The Constancy of Circumstance

As long as my job/marriage/health/finances are secure, I will have peace of mind.

While people who equate peace of mind with absence of conflict move away from what they don't want, people who equate it with 'constancy of circumstance' move toward creating and maintaining the life circumstances they think they need in order to feel relaxed and content.

Though they may think of themselves as 'go-getters' or 'high-achievers,' people chasing constancy of circumstance might more accurately be called 'plate-spinners' or even 'rat-racers.' (Think Willy Loman in *Death of a Salesman*, or any 'supermom' who tries to bring home the bacon, fry it up in a pan and make sure her children have high test scores and early entrance into top universities while never letting her husband forget he's a man.)

Not only is it virtually impossible to sustain peace of mind in every area of our life when we're chasing it from the outside in, but the stress of needing circumstances to conform to our will in a world where life seems to have a mind of its own often takes us further away from peace of mind than we were when we started.

Which is why at some point it's quite common for people to begin to realize that constancy of circumstance is less important than...

3. The Absence of Thought

As long as I don't have too much thinking going on, I'll have peace of mind.

When people make the shift from trying to create peace of mind through external strategies to creating it through quieting thought, life starts to get easier. Because as long as we don't have too much on our mind, we can handle conflict and changes in circumstance much better than your average bear.

People who seek peace of mind by banishing thought are the meditators of the world, and as long as they sustain their practice they tend to live healthier, longer, more creative lives than non-meditators. (Rupert Murdoch, David Lynch, and Oprah Winfrey are some modern-day examples of high-achievers who make time for daily meditation.)

But absence of thought can also lead to dullness of wits, and the difficulty for many people of maintaining their peace of mind in the 23 hours a day when they're not meditating can turn the practice into a chore.

The people who continue to meditate as a 'love to' rather than a 'should' are often those who've experienced...

4. The Peace of Mind

Peace is the nature of Mind.

Mind is the formless energy and intelligence behind life – the life-force that animates our world. It is everywhere and ever-present, and it brings with it a feeling of being alive and a knowing that regardless of what's going on in our head or in our world, all is well.

People who recognize that the peace of Mind surrounds them find themselves dropping into states of meditation, gratitude, and love wherever they are and whatever is happening around them. (Think Jesus, or the Buddha, or modern mystics like Syd Banks, the Dalai Lama, Byron Katie, and Eckhart Tolle.)

When we see that we live in a mind-made world and that we ourselves are of that same formless energy, the idea of having to do anything to experience peace of Mind is as bizarre as the idea that a fish would have to do something to experience water. When you start to notice that the peace of Mind is always present, it begins to fill your consciousness more and more of the time.

Quite simply, the peace of Mind is your true nature. You can never lose it, because it's the very core of your being. As St. Francis of Assisi is reported to have said, 'You are that which you are seeking.'

And the best thing about experiencing the peace of Mind is that it's always available, regardless of who's disappointed in you, what they're disappointed about, and what you happen to be thinking about it at the time.

CHASING A NATURAL HIGH

Of course, once I realized that the peace of Mind was always available, the goal-seeking part of my brain started hunting for ways to experience it more of the time.

'If peace of Mind is a worthy goal,' I said to myself, 'are we better off cultivating the feeling of peace or a deeper understanding of Mind in order to get there?'

Now, I knew that this was a false dichotomy – sort of like trying to make yourself choose between having a face or a stomach – but I was sufficiently intrigued to spend some time letting the question bounce around inside my head.

The first thing I realized was that I'd been asking myself variations on this question for over 30 years, ever since I'd felt the breeze as I was closing the refrigerator door in my parents' kitchen and dropped into a lovely feeling of peace that I've never forgotten.

After my attempts at recreating the feeling by opening and closing refrigerators everywhere I went failed miserably (I really do wish I was joking), I set off on a psycho-spiritual quest to both understand where that feeling of peace came from and how I could experience it more of the time. That search led me to study Zen and other Eastern religions, then spiritual healing and metaphysics, then NLP and positive psychology.

On each step of my journey, I found myself torn between cultivating the feeling directly and gaining a deeper understanding of how life worked in the hope that my understanding would sustain me when that magical feeling of peace next abandoned me.

This apparent dilemma seemed to be alive and well in the work of Syd Banks. In many of his books and recordings he talked about living in a beautiful feeling as both the means and end to a richer life. Yet in many of his later writings and recordings he talked about the importance of understanding the nature of Mind, Consciousness, and Thought as a pathway to the divine – an altogether more intellectual-sounding pursuit and one that appealed to my scientific 'if I can't explain it, it doesn't exist' way of thinking.

So which path to follow? If even the gurus and guides on the path couldn't decide, how could I?

Before I drove myself completely nuts, I took my noisy head for a walk along the beach, turning my attention to the waves and letting my thoughts drift wherever they happened to go. And then, as so often happens, something completely new and fresh came to mind…

If there is a universal Mind behind the spinning of the planets, the order in which wild animals drink at the watering hole, and the beating of the hearts of all who live, then it's probably not my job to figure out what I'm going to want for dinner tomorrow night, let alone how to solve the mysteries of the universe. When and if I need to know, I'll know; if I don't need to know, I probably won't.

Since that time I've found another level of peacefulness, even in the midst of a whole lot of not-so-easy stuff happening in my day-to-day life. The feeling of deep wellbeing seems more stable than it has in the past – less 'easy come, easy go' and more of a touchstone and constant companion.

While reflecting on that fact, I've seen that the difference is one of attribution. In the past, I chalked my periods of peace up to grace – moments of bliss that seemed like gifts from the divine when I was in a more spiritual frame of mind and happy accidents when I wasn't. While I was always grateful for every moment I got to spend in those feelings, it never really felt as though they had anything to do with me – I was either feeling them or I wasn't.

Now, it seems to me that those feelings of peace are the natural effect of seeing that the deeper Mind is always on, 24/7, and that it not only 'has my back,' it's a part of who I am. And when I'm feeling scared and insecure, it's just because I've lost sight of that and gone back to thinking that I'm supposed to be able to handle this whole 'life' thing on my own.

In this sense, the peace of Mind doesn't come and go of its own accord – it's 100 percent responsive to our recognition of the natural order of things. As we see that the only thing we're ever up against is the insecure feeling of our own transient thoughts, dressed up in the clothing of fear and an uncertain world, we also get to see what we're made of: the energy and intelligence of life itself.

It's something like this (but not this):

Imagine living 100 feet above a beautiful lake. Most of the time it doesn't even occur to you to look down, but whenever you do you are struck by the purity, depth, and tranquillity of the water. Every now and again, almost by accident, you drop down into the lake and get soaked, and it is the most refreshing feeling, like drowning in an ocean of love and peace.

Then one day it occurs to you to orient yourself toward the lake deliberately and on a more regular basis. Almost imperceptibly, you begin to drop down closer and closer to the level of the water. As you get closer, you drop down into it more often. Sometimes you just get your toes wet; at other times you go all the way in. But it becomes more familiar, even though it is no less refreshing than before. Soon you can drop down into the lake almost on demand, dipping in and out of it whenever you feel the need to cool down and clean yourself off.

Then one day you realize that you can spend your days floating on the surface of the lake, being supported by its natural buoyancy. Every now and then you slip under and go deep; every now and then you drift up away from the surface. But for the most part you simply rest on the water and enjoy the beauty of the day...

RESTING IN PEACE

For many years I've signed my e-mails with the word 'love' in the final line where 'sincerely' often goes. This was originally a conscious experiment and it has provoked the occasional upset (and in one instance downright hostile) comment from people who feel that love is a somewhat limited commodity which should only be used sparingly lest we use it up and don't have any left for when it really matters.

What I discovered, perhaps unsurprisingly, is that love is one of those renewable resources where the more you give, the more you have to give, and these days I don't give it a second thought. Yet when someone signed off on a recent email to me with the words 'Rest in peace,' I found myself being the one getting upset. Was this a veiled threat? Did they have some insight into my state of health and this was their not so subtle way of letting me know?

It reminded me of one of the first jokes I ever remember hearing:

> *Late one evening, a chaplain goes to an army captain with a dilemma. He's just returned from town, where he's seen the young wife of Private Jenkins kissing and cuddling another man. He doesn't want to be the one to break the news, but he doesn't feel he can keep it to himself either.*

The captain tells him not to worry and that he'll take care of it.

The next morning at muster, while everyone is standing to attention, the captain orders all the happily married men in the unit to take one step forward. As they do so, he calls out, 'Not so fast, Jenkins...'

When my thinking settled, I realized the phrase 'rest in peace' reflected a rather beautiful sentiment and that but for its funereal implications, it was something I would wish for any human being. It also occurred to me that only in an outside-in world, where it appears that our feelings are at the mercy of our circumstances, would it occur to us that we might have to wait until we were dead to 'rest in peace.'

What if we can rest in peace while being fully alive?

The nature of the human experience is that we live in the feeling of our thinking, not the feeling of the world. And peace is our natural state – the space we are born into and seem to notice most often in those moments when we can feel our way beyond the edges of our thinking. So our ability to rest in peace is not a function of how busy our life is or how challenging our circumstances are, it's simply a matter of how often we are willing to pause in the midst of a busy mind and return to the beauty of the present moment.

Better still, peace isn't just a beautiful feeling, it's the space in which anything is possible. It's a gateway to our inner wisdom and the mysteries of the universe. When we rest in peace, our body recharges, our thoughts refresh, and our personal mind synchronizes with something larger and more universal.

Perhaps that's why 'rest in peace' is such a common phrase when someone dies – we intuitively recognize that the separate self has returned to the universal whole from which it came.

Of course I don't know what really happens when we die, though I've read some fascinating accounts from people who've apparently done it and lived to tell the tale. But I do know that it's not only possible to rest in peace while being fully alive, it's one of the most rewarding and ultimately practical ways to live.

Chapter 5

THE SECRET OF EFFORTLESS CHANGE

CHANGE IS NATURAL AND INEVITABLE – IT'S SOMETHING WE RESIST, NOT SOMETHING WE HAVE TO MAKE HAPPEN.

THE LIMITS OF REVERSE ENGINEERING

'Money can buy you a fine dog, but only love can make him wag his tail.'

Kinky Friedman

'Reverse engineering' is a term used to describe the process of taking something apart to see how it works in order to either copy it or improve upon it. While it was traditionally used in the context of manufacturing or computing, there are a growing number of psychological disciplines which attempt to improve certain traits, attitudes, and cognitive abilities by studying people who are already successful in an attempt to 'reverse engineer' these traits and make them more accessible to all of us.

While some of these techniques work wonders for specific outcomes, many of the reverse-engineered 'secrets to change' bear a striking resemblance to what the physicist Richard Feynman called 'Cargo Cult Science.'

In a lecture to a graduating class at Caltech, Feynman said:

> *In the South Seas there is a Cargo Cult of people. During [World War II] they saw airplanes land with lots of good materials, and they want the same thing to happen now. So they've arranged to make things like runways, to put fires along the sides of the runways, to make a wooden hut for a man to sit in, with two wooden pieces on his head like headphones and bars of bamboo sticking out like antennas – he's the controller – and they wait for the airplanes to land.*

> *They're doing everything right. The form is perfect. It looks exactly the way it looked before. But it doesn't work. No airplanes land. So I call these things Cargo Cult Science, because they follow all the apparent precepts and forms of scientific investigation, but they're missing something essential, because the planes don't land.*

In my own early work, I developed a number of techniques which I shared under the somewhat tongue-in-cheek name 'behavioral Prozac,' because it seemed to me that when practiced consistently they helped stave off depression and the extremes of overwhelmingly negative emotion in myself and my clients.

But therein lay the problem. When we most needed the techniques was when we were least inclined to use them, so we then needed additional techniques to motivate us to apply them when we really didn't want to. If those techniques didn't work, I would go out and find or invent new ones.

Which in retrospect is kind of like the witch doctor in the Cargo Cult prescribing coconut shells instead of wooden pieces as headphones when the planes continue not to land. Within the misunderstanding of where cargo comes from, it seems like a reasonable adjustment to make, but when you know where cargo really comes from, it's obviously (and somewhat charmingly) missing the point.

Sitting in a hut by a dirt runway is unlikely to bring an airplane filled with cargo to your tiny island unless you get extremely lucky; copying the behavior spontaneously produced by people who transform their lives will rarely transform yours, though it certainly can shake things up and get your mind off your own repetitive thoughts and behavior.

So what's the solution?

In my experience, the more people look toward their own moments of spontaneous change, the more those moments seem to occur. And when they look beyond what they happened to be thinking or doing at the time to see how change happens and where it comes from, they inevitably notice that it seems to come from nowhere, arriving out of the blue like the sun breaking through clouds on an otherwise gray and blustery day.

HOW EFFORTLESS CHANGE HAPPENS

Frank (not his real name) was a businessman from Europe who came to me to improve his client acquisition skills. During our first session, we talked about the illusory nature of thought and how easy it was to get sucked into believing that it was important to pay attention to and even act upon the seemingly constant noise in our head.

Because I went away on holiday the day after our session, I didn't speak with Frank again for nearly three weeks. When I came back, he asked me how I'd managed to get him to stop biting his fingernails after over 20 years of trying.

Somewhat confused, I reviewed my notes from the session and found that not only had we not spoken about his nail-biting, I hadn't even known it had been an issue for him. Yet I did have an understanding of how a lifelong habit could completely disappear without any particular effort from either of us, miraculous though it might seem.

Here's how I explained it to him:

Imagine living in a world stalked by a hungry dragon. For many of us, our first priority is going to be building a castle to protect ourselves. But what to build the castle out of?

Some people try to use money to build the walls of their castle. 'If only I have enough money,' they think, 'the dragon won't be able to get me and I'll be safe.' They spend their lives desperately earning as much as they can and fearfully spending as little of it as possible, convinced that if they can only accumulate enough, the dragon will never be able to scale the walls.

Others build their castle walls out of approval, adulation, and fame. 'If only people love and respect and admire me enough,' they think, 'the dragon won't be able to get me and I'll be safe.' Each new bit of acclaim is like another stone in the castle wall, while each shot to their reputation is like a battering ram against the gates.

Still others attempt to build their castle walls with sex and intimate relationships ('If I can get just one person to really love me...'), healthy living ('If I just eat all the right things and do all the right things...'), or the pursuit of power and position ('If I can just fight my way to the top...') to keep themselves safe.

But, as you can imagine, not everyone is successful at building and defending their castle, and even those who do well in the world get bitten by the dragon from time to time. And if you haven't been bitten by a dragon before, well ... let's just say it's extremely painful.

So people learn to drink or smoke or eat or gamble or even bite their nails to numb the pain and to mitigate the continual anxiety of having to defend themselves against the dragon, who, as every child knows, could be lurking around every corner or hidden behind the deceptive smile of a stranger posing as a friend.

But what would happen if you woke up one day and realized beyond a shadow of a doubt that there was no dragon? If you could see that what you thought was the dragon's shadow was in fact just the shadow of a thought?

If you really saw that there was no dragon, all your anxiety and stress would dissipate almost immediately. And the cacophony of dragon-avoiding activity would come to an immediate end as well. Nails would no longer need to be bitten (or approval sought or food/money/drugs consumed at a startling rate) if the source of your anxiety was no longer there. In short, you could simply relax and enjoy your life.

Of course things wouldn't always turn out as you hoped, and from time to time you might even see something that looked a bit like a dragon or feel something that hurt as badly as a dragon's bite. But before you could get too caught up in it, something would happen to remind you that you're never afraid of what you think you're afraid of — you're afraid of what you think. And in just a few moments, you would return to your natural state of health and ease and wellbeing...

Frank went on to say that not only was he no longer biting his nails, he was also truly enjoying both his work and his life for the first time in years.

Here's another metaphor for how change happens effortlessly and naturally even when it seems as though we're the ones doing all the work...

Imagine a river covered over with ice. Even though the ice may be many inches thick, the river continues to flow underneath it. Now imagine that your job is to break up the ice and 'free the river' so that it comes back up to the surface and can be seen and enjoyed by all.

Each day, you go down to the river and chip away at the ice. Some days you may break through it in one or two isolated spots; other days you may not have any 'breakthroughs,' but the constant chipping away will have weakened something structural.

While this may seem a frustrating and difficult job, especially if the river has been iced over for a long time and become particularly thick in places, you have a secret ally in your task: the river itself.

At some point in this process, larger chunks of ice will begin to break away and the river will begin to show through more and more. When the ice breaks up enough, the river itself will

> take over the process, as the warmer water and continual flow will remove the remaining ice by both carrying it downstream and enabling it to melt back into the water of which it was originally formed.

At the risk of explaining away the obvious, we all have a deep river of wisdom and wellbeing which has been running through us from the moment we were born. Over time, this river gets iced over in places and we learn to drive ourselves forward on the treacherous 'ice roads' of our psyche instead of flowing along, carried by the river.

What those of us who facilitate transformative conversations do is to chip away at the 'ice' of long-held beliefs and other objectified thoughts while simultaneously 'presencing the river' – speaking to the health and wisdom inside people, drawing it up to the surface more and more.

While there's certainly an element of artistry to our work, in a way it's a very blue-collar job. We clock in at the beginning of each day, do what it occurs to us to do to chip away at the ice and presence the river, and clock out at the end of the day, never knowing at exactly what point the water will break through the ice, reuniting our client's psyche with the spirit out of which it was formed.

But what keeps us showing up for work each day is the absolute certainty that the principles behind the mind are as constant as the principles behind nature. At some point, if we keep chipping away at the ice (and sometimes even if we don't), the river of wisdom and wellbeing will rise to the surface and once again run freely through our client's mind.

[Chapter 6]

A FRESH START

WE ARE DESIGNED TO LIVE
FROM THE INFINITE CREATIVE
POTENTIAL, NOT THE HISTORY
OF OUR PAST CREATIONS.

A WORLD OF PURE POSSIBILITY

'I dwell in possibility.'

Emily Dickinson

What if everything in life was up for grabs and there were no givens?

A number of years ago, I had a client who felt he was being held back in his career by his worry about dying prematurely. It obsessed his thinking and prevented him from making clear decisions about his future in case he wasn't going to be around to see things through.

I was only just beginning to bring the inside-out understanding into my coaching at that point, so we initially looked into his circumstances, making sure he had a full physical examination (he was relatively healthy for a man his age), that his will and life insurance were up to date, and addressing anything else we could think of that might be 'causing' him to worry.

When none of that made any real difference to his level of concern, I offered up what seemed even to me to be somewhat lame advice. 'You don't feel bad about things when you're *not* thinking about dying,' I said, 'so don't think about dying.'

Funnily enough, that helped him more than either of us expected. His head cleared, he became more positive, and things got better.

The next time I had a session with my mentor coach at the time, Sandy Krot, I asked her what she would have said or done in that situation.

'I would have told him, "*You don't have to think about that,*"' she said.

I dutifully wrote down her words of wisdom in my notebook, but I left the session disappointed that she'd come up with pretty much the same lame response as I had.

In our next session together, I brought it up again, arguing that there must be something that could be said or done to improve my client's plight beyond simply telling him to avoid thinking about the situation (regardless of the fact that it seemed to be working).

Sandy looked confused. 'What do you think I said?' she asked.

'I have it written down,' I replied. 'You said that you would say: "You don't have to think about that."'

She smiled. 'That may be what you wrote down, but it's not what I said. I said, *"You don't have to think that."*'

Somehow those six words rocked my world. While the idea that my 'reality' was made up of thought wasn't new to me, for the first time it dawned on me how fluid and changeable that meant my experience of life could be. After all, if I didn't have to continue to think about things the way I'd always thought about them, I was free to create a whole new world for myself.

Things which had previously seemed set in stone were suddenly up for grabs, and I could feel the fabric of my reality dissolving as I wondered things like:

♦ 'Am I really a shy person?'

♦ 'Does taking on big challenges really have to be stressful?'

♦ 'Is death really a bad thing?'

I sat in stunned silence for what felt like hours as all of my previously held notions of how life worked went from solid 'facts' to fluid thoughts, and I was simultaneously scared and excited by the possibilities of living in a completely thought-created reality.

As my thinking began to settle, I saw clearly how valuable it was to have things I could rely on in a world which was in a state of continual flux:

◆ the presence of Mind – an energy and intelligence that acted as both catalyst and guide for the unfolding of life

◆ the fact of Consciousness – a capacity for experience that allowed me to be aware of my reality and brought my thinking to life via the five senses

◆ the gift of Thought – the divine 'play dough' out of which reality was being created and recreated, moment by moment and day by day

I could see and feel at that moment that all any of us are ever suffering from is our innocent misuse of the play dough of Thought. When we use it to create insecurity, worry, and fear, we live inside a cage with bars of our own making. But, like a child who gleefully creates and destroys animals and people and monsters and flowers every time they take their play dough out of its container, we're free to change our mind and think differently about absolutely anything at absolutely any moment.

I don't always remember this, and there are certainly times when my reality becomes very 'real' to me and I feel the walls closing in on my self-created cage. But then a new thought comes along, and I'm once again reminded that I can roll up the bars of my cage into a lump of divinely neutral play dough, change my mind, and begin the game of creation all over again.

THE POWER OF THE BLANK PAGE

I expressed this idea in a seminar recently by making a drawing on a flip chart like this:

If I decide I don't like the drawing, I can try to fix it like this:

But if I still don't like it, then what? Perhaps I might add to it some more, like this:

At some point, I hit a point of diminishing returns, where my attempts to improve the drawing just obscure the original and make it harder and harder to see.

What's the solution?

Turn the page...

At any moment, we can turn the page on our past and begin again. We can make a fresh start. We can move forward as if nothing had happened. We can make things as good as new.

THE MYTH OF 'SADDER BUT WISER'

I used to think forgiveness was the act of letting go of resentment, and I thought it was an excellent idea. In fact I used to love telling people that hanging on to a grudge was like drinking poison and expecting the other person to die. The only problem was, it didn't really help me to know that. While I was never a big grudge-holder, it seemed important to hang on to the resentments I did carry, just in case I found myself in a similar situation sometime in the future.

Then I heard something that I liked even more, which was the notion that in order to forgive, you have to already have judged. So forgiveness is a self-righteous illusion, because I already have to think I know better than you before it even occurs to me to forgive you. So in talking about forgiveness I kind of got to be a jerk twice – first judgmental, then arrogant.

The only reason I didn't give up on forgiveness entirely was that I noticed I found great comfort in the phrase 'All your sins are forgiven.' Even though I didn't know how that would be possible, I really liked the idea of it.

Then one day I was talking to one of my mentors, George Pransky, and he said to me, 'Well, it seems to me that true forgiveness is when you can feel the same way about the person as you did before anything ever happened.'

Now I'd never even considered that as a possibility. By now, I was okay at lessening grudges. I was pretty good at 'I'm going to like you anyways, even though you were wrong.' It hadn't actually occurred to me that there was a deeper possibility for forgiveness – that you could actually go back to how it was before it ever happened. As soon as I heard it, I knew it was true. Better still, I knew it wasn't only true for me in relation to other people, it was true in relation to myself.

'Sadder but wiser' is a misnomer. It usually means 'sadder and more cynical.' When we're feeling low – when we're sad – we're usually listening to the noise of our thinking and oblivious to the whispers of our deeper wisdom. That wisdom is easiest to hear when our mind is at rest.

Most of the time, we're so caught up in our head that we're not noticing the quiet of our mind. There's so much noise from the marching band of our personal thinking that we don't hear the piccolo of wisdom. But when we forgive – when we allow ourselves to hold a person (including ourselves) in the same space of love as we did before that horrible 'unforgiveable' thing that we can never let go of happened – it turns out we're both as perfect and whole as we ever were.

That's the deeper possibility offered by forgiveness: the possibility of a fresh start. In this sense the mind works like a self-cleaning oven. No matter what got burnt in the past, the system resets and the oven doesn't retain any of the flavor or residue of what was cooked in it before. When you go back to it the next time, it's as good as new. That's the nature of the Mind. That's the nature of this infinite creative potential.

In religious terms, this possibility of complete forgiveness – a truly fresh start in life – is often talked about as being 'born again.' Now putting aside the religious connotations for a moment, that sounds horrible to me – sitting around in dirty diapers all day long, having to learn to walk and talk from scratch. But if you think about it metaphorically, wouldn't it be cool to get a second chance at life?

This is what forgiveness actually offers – the chance to start over. Not 'given what's happened to me and what I've done before, here's the best I can hope for,' but an actual honest-to-goodness fresh-from-the-oven new beginning, simply by being willing not to think the thoughts that got you here.

And in the end, that's all forgiveness is. It's just letting go of all the thinking you've got about why life can never be good again, why you're never going to be okay again, why people will never love you again, why you'll never be able to love again, why 'our relationship is irreparably damaged and we'll never be able to be close again.'

The truth is, it's never too late to forgive. It's not too late even when the person you think you need to forgive (or needs to forgive you) is dead. I've seen many people forgive after someone has died, and something heals when they do that. Something that was closed off opens back up, and it's beautiful to see.

That's the true power of forgiveness. What allows it to happen is that we're not our story. We're not our thoughts. We're the infinite creative potential – the space within.

GOING BACK TO THE DRAWING BOARD

This is equally true in the realm of creativity. When I first began doing radio shows for Hay House Radio over 10 years ago, I thought we'd have a shelf life of about three months before my bag of tricks was empty and people (including me) would start losing interest. My first attempt at addressing this problem was to expand my bag of tricks and put more tools into my toolbox, and I began reading at an ever more voracious pace to keep my head continually filled with whatever was at the cutting edge of psycho-spiritual thought.

Before each show, I'd print off up to a dozen pages of tips and techniques so I had something to fall back on if not enough people phoned in for me to talk with. But then one week I got to the studio late and didn't have time to print anything off for 'just in case.' For the first time, I'd forgotten my toolbox and didn't have my bag of tricks with me. To my surprise, the show not only went well, it went considerably better than many of my prepared shows.

Here's what I realized that day:

You don't need a toolbox or a bag of tricks if you have access to a well.

Once you see that the infinite well of creativity (i.e., the deeper Mind) is always available to you, all you need to do is empty your mind, drop your bucket into that well, and see what comes up. If you don't like it, you don't have to drink it – you can dip your bucket back into the well as often as you like.

It takes a load off your mind when you don't have to carry what you've done before around with you everywhere you go. And each time you get fresh new ideas from the creative well, you trust it a little bit more and you get more of a feel for letting things come to you in that way. It's not only easier, it's more fun, and it's surprising how often what comes through is the perfect solution for the task at hand.

As I got more and more comfortable just showing up for each broadcast and being open to whatever showed up, I began to see that what was happening was completely in line with the nature of creativity. Form always comes out of the formless; everything is created from nothing. So whether I was brainstorming possibilities, doing a show, or writing a book or article, the more willing I was to hang out in the unknown and show up with a clean slate, an empty bucket, and a blank piece of paper, the more likely it was that something fresh and new would come through me and out into the world.

In fact, when I got stuck and insecure about not having anything to say, it was inevitably because I was trying to repurpose an old idea instead of just hanging out in the infinite creative potential of the Mind.

And that's true in every area of our life. In any situation, we have the choice to either show up empty-handed and fully present or already full of what we think we know and what we've done before. But every time we do it the way we've done it before, it feels a little bit staler. Our stories start to sound like stories, our pitch feels as though we've made it a million times, and we start to have to work at making things *seem* fresh instead of allowing them to actually *be* fresh.

Whereas if you're willing to go back to the drawing board every single time, you know that things will never get dull.

You won't get into a rut, or start dreading the fourth meeting of the day, because every single time you're starting with a clean slate, an empty bucket, and a blank piece of paper.

And the best thing of all is that it doesn't even matter if you're not terribly fond of what you create. Because you're always creating from nothing, you can wipe the slate clean, empty the bucket, crumple up the paper, and start again.

It's something like this (but not this):

Imagine that from the moment we're born, every one of us is given our own magical cow as a companion. Any time we need nourishment, we need only look to the cow and it will give us fresh milk. Being a magical cow, its milk is healing, delicious, and nourishing, giving even the most lactose-intolerant among us exactly what we need to function beautifully moment by moment.

Now imagine that over time we forget about our magical bovine companion but never lose our craving for its milk. We seek to slake our thirst from the cows of those around us, even arguing with others about where to find the 'one true cow' that will deliver unto us the freshest, most nourishing milk.

We might even be tempted to go down to the village every Sunday and stockpile a week's supply of our favorite brand, so that if we find ourselves in need of extra nourishment in the midst of our day-to-day life, we always have some to hand. Yet this bottled milk rarely refreshes us in the way that it did when we first drank it, and no matter how wonderful the farmer whose cow gave us the milk, it never quite delivers the magical quality of perfect nourishment that our own cow's fresh milk contains.

Some of us might even carry around bottles of the milk that had nourished us as children, dismissing its sour taste as a function of our own unworthy taste buds and not as a function of what happens to all milk when it's been away from its source for too long.

Finally, imagine waking up one morning and remembering that having a magical cow as a companion is your birthright as a human being — a gift from the divine to remind you of your spiritual nature, even as you live your one and only life fully in the world. You look into its soft eyes and realize it has never left you, and you feel deep gratitude for its presence in your life.

Sure, you might still enjoy tasting the milk from other cows, but you cease to look to it for nourishment. Carrying around old milk looks less and less of a good idea, and once again you come to rely on your own magical companion as the source of exactly what you need exactly when you need it...

Chapter 7

THE KEY TO HIGH PERFORMANCE

THE LESS YOU HAVE ON YOUR
MIND, THE HIGHER YOUR
LEVEL OF PERFORMANCE.

MOJO

In the movie *Austin Powers: The Spy Who Shagged Me*, Dr. Evil attempts to thwart the heroic title character by stealing his 'mojo.' And apart from the fact that mojo is invisible to the eye and can't actually be stolen by anyone else, this is a fantastic evil plan. Because when a person has their mojo working, anything is possible; when it's not, they struggle to get out of bed in the morning and even more to take on the challenges and opportunities of the day.

While the dictionary tells us that 'mojo' originally referred to a magical charm bag used in African hoodoo, it also defines it as follows:

Mojo (n)

[**moh**-joh]

noun

1. a power that may seem magical and that allows someone to be very effective, successful, etc.

In my work unleashing the human potential with people from all walks of life, I see the impact of this kind of natural confidence play out in every facet of our lives. When we have our mojo working, we can move mountains; when we lose our mojo, the mountains seem to be three times the height, and the possibility they might be moved doesn't even occur to us.

Fortunately, we can't really 'lose' our mojo because it isn't really a magical power – it's a description of the feeling we get when we're conscious of the intelligence and energy of spirit running through us. When we're in touch with that invisible energy, we're 'live wires,' filled with power and capable of creating sparks of inspiration and lighting up whatever we touch.

The *feeling* of 'losing our mojo' comes when we get caught up in our thinking and lose touch with that connection to source. It's like unplugging from the mains and running on battery power instead. At first we might not notice the difference – the screen dims a bit, things turn off more quickly, and some functions are disabled to preserve battery life – but over time, as our batteries get really run down, we're operating with so little power we can barely keep the lights on, let alone light up the world.

If you're trying to achieve great things with your life, chances are you know that feeling all too well. You're doing your best, but you're doing it on spit and vinegar instead of gasoline and motor oil. Instead of a V-8 engine, you've got a squirrel on a wheel chasing a peanut under the hood. Sure, the system is still up and running, but only at a level which allows you to stay the course. There's just not enough power available to break through and move forward. It feels as though you're on your own and the only way something is going to happen is if you make it happen, running on 5 percent battery and hoping you can get everything done before you run out of juice.

But the only reason you ever feel powerless is because you're out of touch with the deeper Mind. And no matter how long you've been running on battery power and no matter how run down you think you are, the moment you plug back into the mains normal service will be resumed. Everything begins working as designed, and you regain access to all the features.

That's what 'finding your mojo' really is – finding your way back home and plugging back into the universal Mind. The moment you do, you'll notice your apparent problems shrinking down to size. You're running on full power even while your system is recharging. You feel whole again, and your capacity to handle whatever life sends your way with creativity, ease, and grace returns to the natural factory preset.

HOW THE SYSTEM ACTUALLY WORKS

One of the things that bogs us down when it comes to understanding human performance is a fundamental confusion between what is innate and what is a skill that needs to be learned and practiced in order to be usefully implemented in the world.

For example, resilience – the ability to bounce back from any setback – is both natural and built into the human system. As any six-month-old baby would tell you (if they could talk, obviously), no matter how upset you are and no matter how big a tantrum you're throwing, you're only one thought or good cuddle away from returning to the quiet and peace of the space within. We adults, however, tend to think of resilience as a skill we have to develop if we want to let go of the upsets and tantrums that many of us have been nurturing for years.

Like resilience, wellbeing, confidence, learning, and creativity are already built into the human system. They're as natural a part of how we're designed to operate as plants turning sunlight into energy and the human body turning food into fuel. By way of contrast, building a business, playing the piano, coaching a sport, and even writing books are not things that we're either intrinsically good at or not – they're learnable skills that will develop given time, effort, instruction, and practice.

Because most of us confuse what's normal with what's natural, we struggle along in first or second gear most of the time, maybe even happily thinking that 30 miles per hour is as fast as a car is meant to go. But as we gain a better understanding of how cars actually work, we come to realize that instead of pushing the engine harder and harder in a low gear, we can simply shift to a higher one. We'll get better performance and reach higher speeds with less wear and tear on the engine and parts.

When it comes to human performance, that 'gear shift' starts to happen automatically as we learn a bit more about how the system works. Almost without noticing, we begin to get far more done with far less effort.

In traditional coaching, that gear shift is often explained with some version of this formula:

performance = capacity + information

If that were true, the only thing between you and optimal performance would be a missing piece of information. Once you knew what to do, you would get the most out of your innate capacity.

But even a cursory glance at our own life will show up the fallacy in that idea. How many 'strategies for success' have we studied in our lifetime? How much of what we know do we actually apply? Are our results commensurate with what we know, or do they seem to have more to do with what we actually do?

The actual formula for high performance looks more like this:

performance = capacity – interference

In other words, when we eliminate interference, we perform closer to our full capacity. But in order to eliminate interference, we first have to understand what it is and where it comes from.

Here's a visual representation of how our mind functions when we've got our mojo working – in the zone and on our game:

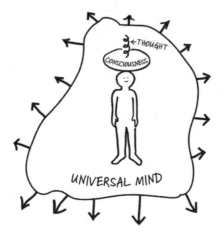

When we're operating in sync with our natural design, we're tuned in and receptive to the infinite potential of the universe (Mind). We're able to experience the energy of the universe taking form (Thought) via an aperture that is continually expanding and contracting (Consciousness).

To function at our absolute best, all we need to do is allow the system to operate as designed. Thought takes form in our personal consciousness as fresh ideas, creative possibilities, loving thoughts, and a moment-by-moment sense of direction, and we move forward in absolute harmony with the intelligence of the universe made manifest via our common sense and a sort of 'wisdom within.'

What could possibly interfere with such a great design?

Well, the problem with a brain is that over time it starts to produce lots and lots of repetitive 'personal thinking' over and above whatever 'fresh-from-the-cow thinking' we really need to perform at our best. Since our experience of life is really an experience of Thought, the more we have on our mind, the more complicated everything seems, and the more the aperture of our consciousness tends to contract. Before we know it, all we can see when we look out into the world is our own thinking reflected back to us in the fun-house mirror of our own self-consciousness.

Where we get ourselves into real trouble is when we then start analyzing and attempting to control our thinking. In the process, we completely lose sight of both the power of Thought and the intelligence of the deeper Mind that can guide us through life with relative ease if we let it.

It looks something like this (but not this):

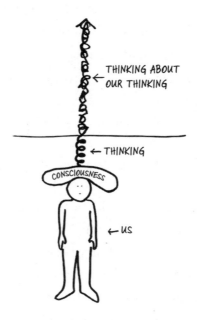

Simply put, the less we have on our mind, the higher our level of performance. The more we have on our mind, the more we're prone to behave like a bit of a mor(e)on...

Here's how I explain it to my clients:

You were born in the zone. From the time you were an infant, you naturally learned about life through present—moment instinct and intuition. You followed your fascination not because 'curiosity is a positive human trait' but because you were genuinely interested in results and what it would take to achieve them.

You didn't learn to walk because you thought it was important, you learned to walk because there was somewhere you wanted to get to and walking seemed to be a good way to get there. You didn't learn to talk because you thought it would make you appear more intelligent, you learned to talk because there was something you wanted to express or request and that seemed to be the best way to do it.

And you learned quickly and you practiced tirelessly and you didn't get bogged down in your 'failures' for one simple reason: you didn't think about them. Which points us to the number one source of 'interference' that limits the amount of time we spend in the zone and on our game:

> We get caught up in our personal thinking
> and we lose our bearings.

Recognizing that this is the only real obstacle you have to overcome is half the battle won. The other half is even simpler:

You don't need to control your thoughts to be free of them.

When you see that your experience of life is thought created, those thoughts begin to lose their hold on you. It's like waking up inside a dream, or becoming conscious of the movie theater when you've been caught up in a movie.

You don't need to do anything about it – the drama of your thinking fades into the background and you find yourself once more in the zone, on your game, and doing exactly what needs to be done to perform at your best and create the results you desire...

[Chapter 8]

LIVING A GUIDED LIFE

IT IS POSSIBLE AT ANY MOMENT
TO ALIGN THE PERSONAL MIND
WITH THE DIVINE MIND.

DOWNLOADING WISDOM

'Do you have the patience to wait until your mud settles and the water is clear? Can you remain unmoving until the right action arises by itself?'

Lao Tzu

One of the coolest things I ever saw at the movies was the scene in *The Matrix* where Neo asks Trinity if she can fly a helicopter. Her response is 'Not yet' – and then she closes her eyes and receives a download from outside the matrix that allows her not only to fly the helicopter but also to wreak some havoc on the evil machines in the process.

A few years after the movie came out, I watched a special-release DVD edition with 'philosopher commentary' by Ken Wilber and Dr. Cornel West. It was heartening to know that at least some of the film's impact was down to carefully researched themes which echoed the wisdom traditions of the perennial philosophy, even if the rest of its success might be attributed to sexy androgynous actors in shiny leather outfits doing cool things with machine guns on Ducati motorcycles.

In short, while the movie was pure fantasy, the notion that people live in a 100 percent thought-created reality largely unaware that there is a world beyond their personal thinking is pure spiritual fact. And while I have yet to receive an instant download enabling me to fly a helicopter, or do brain surgery on an epileptic lemur, the way I live my life is almost entirely dependent on this particular capacity of the mind.

Here's a visual of how the principles behind the human experience work together with our brain to create our experience of life:

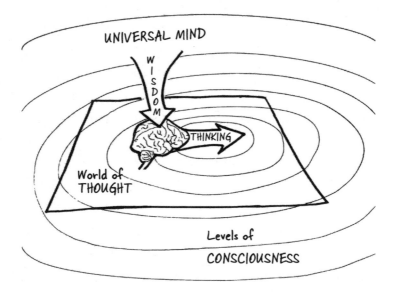

With a limited view, we're only aware of our own thinking, and it appears to us as objective truth, even though it only exists in our own thoughts. Then, as we expand into another level of consciousness, we become aware of the subjective nature of our thoughts, which are often different from other people's thoughts. Expand further, and we become aware of two different kinds of thought – the ones that come from our brain (i.e., memory and received knowledge) and the ones that seem to download into our brain (i.e., inspiration, intuition, and wisdom).

An even deeper understanding reveals that we live in a world of Thought – that in fact we're not designed to experience anything else. This is the first real recognition that things are definitely not what they seem, no matter how real they look, taste, smell, sound, and feel. Beyond this 'human matrix' is the universal Mind – the living intelligence behind life itself.

In more than 25 years spent working with high-achievers, I've noticed that the people who consistently thrive have somehow stumbled across this capacity. They've learned to switch off their personal thinking just enough to open up the space for a deeper guidance to come through. It happens in the shower, at the gym, driving into work, on walks in nature, or sipping coffee in a café. For some, it's a more formal ritual – a meditation practice in a darkened room, or a prayer to a higher power and a surrender of individual will in favor of divine guidance.

What is consistent is that these people have learned or intuitively realized that while factual questions (*'How do I get to Carnegie Hall?' 'What's the boiling temperature of water?'*) can be searched in a database, more open questions (*'How do we grow the company quickly without overextending ourselves?' 'What shall we do about the Middle East?' 'Who am I really and how shall I live?'*) are best answered from a deeper part of the mind.

Here's what I've seen for myself:

> **The moment I turn my attention inward and allow my thoughts to wander, fresh new thinking begins to come through.**

It isn't always brilliant and it isn't always wise, but the more I look to my inner wisdom for guidance, the more often I know exactly what to do next.

DOING WITHOUT A DOER

As well as being a great mentor to me in this work, George Pransky has also become a dear friend. One of my favorite 'George stories' is about a time when he brought a new intern with him to a corporate mediation. The first session was disastrous, with everyone shouting everyone else down and George's counsel being largely ignored.

During the first break, the intern came up to him and said, 'That was awful!'

George replied, 'I know – it really was!'

'What are you going to do?' asked the intern, revved up into a minor panic.

'I don't know yet,' said George calmly, 'but we've got about 20 minutes – hopefully something will come to me during the break.'

At the end of the break, the intern returned. 'Have you figured out what you're going to do?'

'No, nothing's come to me yet.'

'But what are you going to do?'

'I don't know.'

The intern was exasperated. 'You've got to do *something* – they've paid us a fortune and they're all waiting on you!'

George looked surprised. 'What do you want me to do – make something up?'

George wasn't unduly panicked because he knew two things that the intern had yet to discover. The first was that stress and pressure weren't conducive to creative innovation. The second was that inner knowing was both inevitable and inevitably worth waiting for.

This is the mind at its best – operating in the clarity of knowing or not knowing without the infinite shades of gray that come with trying to force an answer or 'make things happen.'

Before coming across the Three Principles, I'd experienced occasional moments of absolute clarity about what was next in my life. Moving to England in the late eighties to go to drama school was a 'no-brainer'; giving up on a successful career and moving back to the US more than a decade later was equally obvious to me (though my wife thought I'd gone a bit nuts). But in between those all too rare moments of clarity, I was wracked with doubt. I lived with a fairly constant feeling of 'background stress,' struggling to make even basic decisions and figure out my best path.

As I learned more about the inside-out understanding and came to see the black-and-white nature of the mind, I realized that all the stress and struggle I'd been experiencing wasn't because I didn't know what to do: it was the effect of thinking I was supposed to be able to figure my life out with my little brain and its limited information and experience.

As I came to see that I could rely on a deeper, more impersonal intelligence – what some might call 'intuition' or 'guidance' or 'inner knowing' – the idea of trying to force an answer and operate under high levels of self-induced pressure and stress seemed like less and less of a good idea.

Over time, it became apparent to me that there were three things about the mind that I could absolutely rely on:

1. When I know, I know. When I don't know, I don't know.

2. There is a deeper wisdom available to me at all times which I can hear most easily when I'm in a settled, reflective state of mind.

3. I know that I'll know when I know.

Now, to the extent that I see the first thing, I dive in when I know and don't try to make myself seem smarter than I am when I don't know.

To the extent that I see the second thing, I relax in the face of the unknown and simply stay in the game until an answer appears.

And to the extent that I see the third thing, I have the patience to stay outside the world of pressure and struggle that gets created when I think I'm supposed to know something before I do.

FORGETTING TO REMEMBER

I heard recently that Syd Banks once ruefully told a friend, 'I always tell people to look within – but they never do!'

Which raises an important question:

> *Given that we all love and value the*
> *richness, deeper feelings, and wisdom*
> *that come from living from the deeper*
> *Mind, why don't we do it all the time?*

This is something I've wrestled with for a number of years in my own life, especially as I've gone further and further along this path. Here's what it seems like to me:

Imagine that you're the pilot of a small spaceship patrolling the asteroid fields in the Gamma quadrant. Since you first took the job you've been hearing rumors about an unusually large asteroid known only as XCF-531, said to be made of a rare mineral with exceptional healing properties. Some of the stories told about this asteroid are of almost epic proportions. There are tales of ancient civilizations which built their homes on it and intrepid explorers who somehow found their way there centuries before space travel was even invented.

Of course you go to check it out at your first opportunity, but to your disappointment it looks a lot like any other asteroid –

barren, rocky, and desolate – and you chalk the stories up to the overactive imagination of a superstitious populace.

Then one day your patrol takes you back into the vicinity of XCF-531 and you decide to take a closer look. The moment you bring your ship into the asteroid's orbit, you feel a strangely peaceful, almost sleepy feeling descending upon you. You immediately check to see if the oxygen levels in your ship have dropped, but you find that all systems within the ship are stable.

As you settle into orbit, you look down and, to your amazement, what seemed from a distance to be a barren desert appears rich with life. The entire asteroid seems to be alive, and you can almost hear the hum of that life over the roar of your spaceship's engines.

You check the ship's readings and find to your surprise that the asteroid's atmosphere will support human life, so you decide to ignore protocol and beam yourself down to the surface. Although you know you should be afraid to be heading out into the unknown, you feel surprisingly calm, as though every cell in your body is telling you that all is well.

What happens next is a bit of a jumble. The first thing you notice is the feeling – a kind of blissful energetic buzz that you normally associate with the sweet emptiness of the moment when you first wake up, before the cares of the day find their way back into your head. Soon you get used to the feeling and the sleepiness is replaced by a remarkable sense of ease and clarity. Your senses seem heightened, and there appears to be an almost visible life—force emanating from the thriving ecosystem on the asteroid's surface.

As you enjoy breathing in the richly oxygenated atmosphere, you can feel your body rejuvenating as it rests in healing bliss. With your renewed sense of mental clarity, you find yourself just knowing things you've wondered about for ages, and you imagine how much better your life would be if you could only live it with this level of mental alertness and profound wellbeing.

Too soon, it's time to return to your ship, and you resolve that not only will you come back daily, but that you will share the healing properties of what you have felt and seen with the entire universe so that no one need ever suffer again.

As you leave the asteroid's orbit, excited about sharing your findings with others, you don't even notice the feelings of wellbeing slipping away and the cares of the world taking their place. In fact, the further away you get from the asteroid, the more the whole experience feels like a dream. Surely that life—force that you thought you saw was just an optical illusion, and even if the asteroid could sustain life, it couldn't possibly have had the healing effect you had imagined...

You decide not to report what you saw to your colleagues lest they think you've gone a bit 'woo woo' from spending too much time on your own, and before long you carry on with your patrols as before, only occasionally thinking back to the beautiful feelings you felt while orbiting XCF-531 and wondering what it would be like to return...

WAITING FOR MISSION CONTROL

I was sitting in the Ivy Club in central London a few months back with a group of my hard-core students, all of whom had spent at least a year of their lives traveling around the world with me sharing this understanding with pretty much anyone who would listen. We were having lunch in the library, sitting around an old oak table in a beautiful art deco room laughing at the fact that while we all had lives to get on with, none of us had any particular personal goals we were scrambling to achieve.

As I looked around the room, I got an image of a bunch of RAF pilots sitting around over coffee between missions during World War II, knowing that at some point they would be called in to fly but with absolutely no say in what that mission would be and relatively little influence (beyond their own presence and skill) over how things would turn out.

For those pilots, the job was simply to be available for the next mission and, when it arrived, to get in the plane and fly it as best they could. Which struck me as a perfect metaphor for living a guided life.

We hang out in the unknown, not knowing what's coming next but not particularly worried about it. We know something will show up, because something always does. The next mission will become apparent, either because it presents itself to us from outside or it occurs to us on the inside. None of it is riding on our shoulders. The next person will come into our life. The next opportunity will knock. When it's time, it'll be time, and we'll get in our planes and fly.

There's something really lovely about both that feeling and that knowing. And it's the very essence of living in and from the deeper Mind...

[Chapter 9]

ALWAYS ALREADY HOME

RESTING IN YOUR TRUE
NATURE IS THE KEY TO PRETTY
MUCH EVERYTHING.

DEFINING PROGRESS

'There is always nowhere to go. You are already home. You are always already home.'

Ramana Maharshi

Having now shared the principles behind the inside-out understanding for nearly a decade, I've found that one of the questions that comes up regularly in a number of different ways from students, clients, and practitioners is: 'If I'm living in the experience of my thinking, not the experience of the outside world, how do I know if I'm making progress?'

While on the one hand I'm not aware of any official benchmarks for 'progress' on the pathless path, there are a few markers and touchstones that I've found to be reliably helpful with my clients and on my own journey through the world of Mind, Consciousness, and Thought:

1. Is It More Fun Being You?

I was speaking about this with Cheryl Bond, a Three Principles-based practitioner with years of experience in the corporate world, and she mentioned that one of the things she had learned to ask people who were wondering if they were really getting anything of value from what they were learning was: 'Is it more fun being you?'

If it is, chances are you're letting go of old thinking and spending more time at home in the space within, enjoying the flow of your wisdom and wellbeing. If not, chances are that you've lost sight of the quiet and been caught back up in the noise and the Three Principles have become one more thing to think about and one more set of rules to be followed.

For myself, I've noticed that my honest answer to the question 'How are you?' has become fairly consistently 'Wonderful!' My life continues to have its ups and downs, as do my feeling states, yet none of that seems to impinge on my essential wonder-filled experience of being alive. And paying attention to that fact seems to matter at a very deep level of experience. As I used to say in my training brochures, 'Wouldn't it be a shame to have a wonderful life and not notice?'

2. Gratitude and Grace

During a recent coaching session, a client commented that she'd been experiencing more 'gratitude and grace' in her life. She was feeling extremely grateful for all the good in her life; she was also finding herself able to handle life's bumps and bruises more gracefully.

This resonated with me as someone who had spent years caught up in the superstitious thought that feeling grateful made me somehow more vulnerable to loss, as if the very act of appreciation would draw the attention of the gods and what I loved most would be taken away from me.

These days, as best I can tell, the 'gods' don't seem to have an opinion about how much I love and appreciate my life and everything in it. And seeing that the only thing I'm ever truly vulnerable to is my own insecure or fearful thinking has allowed me to love more fully and step out into the world with more confidence and grace than ever before.

3. Depth, Purity, and Duration

Throughout this book, I've been using the metaphor of 'coming home' to point to the space which seems to open up inside us as our mind gets quieter and our thoughts begin to flow more freely. In *The Inside-Out Revolution*, I describe the experience of home like this:

We all have within us a deeper essence that's untouched by conditioning and circumstances. We could call this part of us 'the light within' or 'the inner flame' and it's the source of our fundamental sense of inspiration, crackle, and aliveness. Some of my clients have called it their 'twinkle' – the spark of life inside them that appears as a twinkle in the eye on the outside.

This inner glow is made of pure Consciousness, but when we get caught up in the dream of thought, we get cut off from it. Most of us don't notice this disconnection at first, except as a vague sense of something not being quite right. Work just isn't as fulfilling as it once was, our partner isn't quite as handsome or beautiful or loving as we thought they were, and don't even get us started on what might be wrong with us...

Because we've been conditioned from birth to believe in the myth of an outside-in world, we assume the path back to wellbeing and joy and peace of mind must be through getting a better job or a better partner or working on becoming a better person. The irony is that the harder we work on changing ourselves in order to change the way we feel, the more distant we become from our true self, and the more important it seems to work on all those things, and the more lost we become.

So, regardless of what 'problem' we think we have, our only real problem is feeling cut off from our innate wisdom and

*wellbeing. And the moment we reconnect to that source
energy, our problems stop being so problematic and we move
into a new reality.*

Each time we come home to our innate wisdom and
wellbeing, our experience of life gets easier. Instead of
trudging downstream barefoot on a rocky riverbed with a
boat balanced precariously on our head, we allow the river
of life to flow, hop into the boat, and enjoy the ride. We
don't even need to wait to see where that river will take us.
Because the moment we get on board, we're already home.

So what does this all mean?

Simply that 'progress from the inside out' can't be measured
by achieving an external goal or scoring ourselves higher
on each category of the wheel of life. It's about spending
more time in our wellbeing, moving gracefully and gratefully
through life, and increasing the depth, purity, and duration
of our connection to our essential self – the space within.

PUTTING WORDS TO THE MUSIC

When people begin to experience the space within for
themselves, there is a natural desire to share the experience
with others. But they are often surprised at how difficult it
can be to communicate what they are experiencing. As the
philosopher Friedrich Nietzsche is reputed to have said,

'Those who danced were thought insane by those who could not hear the music.' But that difficulty pales in comparison to how much richer their own understanding and experience become in the process.

It's something like this (but not this):

> **When you learn about the principles behind the inside-out understanding, you become more and more attuned to the music of life; when you begin to share them with others, you learn to put words to the music.**

One of the most beautiful articulations of that phenomenon came in the words of Marina Galan, a student on our 'Supercoach Academy' program who now runs programs of her own sharing the inside-out understanding with underprivileged children in Mexico. I encourage you to take your time reading it so that you can hear the music underneath her words:

Go deeper.
For if we do,
Our spirits will embrace
And interweave.
Our union will be so glorious
That even God
Will not be able to tell us apart.
HAFIZ

When I think about the transformative conversation that I was a part of, the first thing that comes to mind is an image of Michael Neill holding a Post-It note in his hand with the word 'HOME' written on it. It was the very first day of our time together, and he was very seriously stating that the journey was all about 'coming home.' I remember a nice feeling falling over the room as we all got quiet and imagined what that could mean.

Throughout the program, we became more trusting of ourselves, of others, of our surroundings, and of life itself. The entire world became more of a home, and the experience of it a most exciting, delightful – and completely safe – adventure.

But it was the last days of the program that really allowed me to begin to understand the scope of those first words Michael said.

As the inevitable end drew nearer, I could see people preparing for goodbyes but I noticed something strange: there was no sense of departing, not a trace of the mourning or nostalgia that inevitably comes when we 'leave' home.

In fact there was no sense of leaving anything behind at all. Nothing. Quite the contrary: our hands and hearts were full to the brim and overflowing, and there was nothing to be left behind and nowhere to leave anything. Whatever had happened, whatever had come to be, it was all coming with us.

And that was when it hit me: it was not the program, Michael and his staff, the other participants, or even the sum of what I had learned that had grown into a sense of home, it was me. I had become Home, along with every single one of us. We all became Home in the widest – and wildest – possible sense:

♦ Through the ability to actually see ourselves and others, we had become a home to them, a safe harbor for them to rest, unfold, and hopefully even see themselves.

♦ Through the recognition of an inner space to which we instinctively return, reverting the usual inertia to look outside for identification and validation, we had become home to ourselves as individuals.

♦ Through the understanding of the fact that our only possible 'ideal self' was actually our very simple, very present, very divine Self, we had become home to our true Selves.

♦ Through the revelation of our inevitable oneness with everything that is, we had become home to a sole ever-expanding Consciousness.

♦ And through the acceptance of ourselves as manifestations of never-ending, ever-growing possibilities, we had become home to the entire Universe.

You see, the invitation in this conversation is not for the 'you' you think you are. The invitation is for the true You, and every minute you spend in the transformative conversation, it is that You who is being summoned. Any mask or disguise you bring to cover the miracle You are is oh so graciously ignored.

But You? You are celebrated to a point where you simply no longer want anything else. And if you follow that impulse to shed what You are not, then you see how, at every moment, life is carefully, lovingly creating Itself for and through You, and that there is no bliss that can come close to actually experiencing this new, miraculous existence where there is nothing left but HOME.

SOME FINAL THOUGHTS...

'The mind exists so we can listen to God.'

Syd Banks

There is a wonderful moment on nearly every course I run where the people attending have their first insight into the inside-out, spiritual nature of life. This insight is often characterized by a quieting of the mind, a feeling of peace and wellbeing in the body, and a light from somewhere deep inside showing up as a twinkle and a smile.

In fact, this happens with such regularity that the first question my wife asks me when I come up from a coaching session for tea is 'Have they "popped" yet?' in the same way that popcorn will reliably yet unpredictably pop whenever it's heated.

When they've popped (and even when they haven't), it's not uncommon for people to imagine what it will be like to go back into their busy lives and take their new insights and sense of clarity and wellbeing out for a spin.

The problem with these daydreams about the future, as I have come to learn, is that when you experience a fundamental shift in your understanding of life, there's no way to predict how a situation will seem to you the next time you come upon it. Things that in the past might have appeared as 'difficult' or even 'crises' may now not even seem significant. I've even had clients complain that they couldn't tell how impactful our time together had been because the 'difficult people' in their life had become uncharacteristically helpful or that they had had an unusually quiet and low-key month at work or at home.

This makes sense when you consider what a spiritual life actually is:

A spiritual life is a life infused with spirit.

How might that look? It might look like a lot of time spent in prayer or meditation or on long walks in nature. It might look like a lot of time spent at work with a quiet smile on your face. At times, it might look like the epitome of success; at other times, it might look like the fresh start of bankruptcy or divorce.

In other words, because spirit infuses our lives from the inside out, we can live a spiritual life without anything having to change in our circumstances or behavior. Changes will happen, but they will tend to happen of their own accord, without any particular act of will or effort on our part.

I once had a conversation with an incredibly sincere student who took exception to the idea that waking up to our spiritual nature and living a spirit-infused life was a more highly leveraged shift than directly helping someone with their apparent problems.

'I don't know about you,' he said, 'but if someone comes to me with a broken leg, I'm going to fix their leg before I talk with them about their spiritual nature!'

'I'd like to think that I would too,' I replied, 'but I can tell you that in my experience, once you start to see the world through the eyes of spirit, you'll notice a lot fewer people have broken legs than you thought.'

I wish you well in every aspect of your life, and may the light within you illuminate the world around you.

With all my love,

Michael

RESOURCES

Since *The Inside-Out Revolution* came out in 2013, the field of the Three Principles has spread through the world at a rate that is positively revolutionary!

New books and resources are being released every single month and in multiple languages.

To find an up-to-date list of resources (including all of Syd Banks' available books, DVDs, and audio recordings), please visit www.michaelneill.org/resources

PERMISSIONS

The author and publisher would like to thank the following for permission granted to reproduce copyright material in this book:

ACKNOWLEDGMENTS

From time to time, I ask my students to reflect on how many people it takes to make a peanut butter sandwich. This seems like an easy question until you realize that somewhere along the line a farmer has to plant the wheat and peanuts, a glass or plastic manufacturer has to mold the jar, a cutler has to set to work on the knife, and a potter on the plate. Similarly, it is impossible to calculate the number of people who contribute to the creation of a book. So, while I will do my best to acknowledge many of the key players in this one, know that I'm only scratching the surface of the debt of gratitude I owe to others.

I'll begin with my agent, Robert Kirby, and the Hay House team led by Michelle Pilley, Reid Tracy, and Margarete Nielsen. Without your incredible belief in what I do and patience with me while I do it, none of this would happen. This is the fourth book I've done with my editor Lizzie Henry, and it is largely thanks to her pedantic bloody-mindedness (rivaling my own) that so few of my mistakes make it into print. (Please know that she took this as a great compliment, except to point out that I'd left out the hyphen between 'bloody' and 'mindedness'.) Similar thanks to Julie Oughton and Leanne Siu Anastasi for their help with the look and feel of the book, and in particular to my best friend, David Beeler, for the illustrations and to Randy Stuart for another wonderful cover. I don't speak 'visual,' so your ability to translate my mental pictures into form is a godsend.

Next up is my team at michaelneill.org: Joe and Terri Alamo, Sara Murre, Lynne Robertson, and Annette Watling. Without your commitment to providing the structures and support for the inside-out community, most of what I do would never make it out into the world. Special mention to my long-time business manager, Michelle Walder – someday I will figure out what I did in a past life to deserve your generosity and kindness, and when I do, I will find a way to go back in time and pat myself on the back for it.

A surprise (well, to me anyways) thank-you to Microsoft for developing the Surface Pro 4. My old laptop died in the middle of writing this book, and were it not for the ease of getting up and running on a new machine and the fun of getting to play with the Surface Pen, this book might have been abandoned and would certainly never have had any illustrations in it.

My teachers and mentors in this understanding are legion, but I will do my best to make an alphabetical list of those who have taken the time to work with me along the way and whose understanding is no doubt reflected in this book:

Thanks to Joseph and Michael Bailey, Dicken Bettinger, Keith Blevens, Cheryl Bond, Robin Charbit, Chip and Jan Chipman, Don Donovan, Mara Gleason, Mark Howard, Robert Kausen, Sandy Krot, Ken Manning, Kristen Mansheim, Gabriela Maldonado-Montano, Leslie Miller, Ami Chen Mills-Maim, Valda Monroe, Bill Pettit, Jack Pransky, Linda Pransky, Shaul Rosenblatt, Terry Rubenstein, Judith Sedgeman, and Aaron Turner. Special thanks to Michele Christensen for letting me borrow your blessing – your light has been illuminating the world around you for all the years I've known you and will no doubt continue to do so for generations to come. A special thank-you as well to Cathy Casey for helping me find the courage to go ahead with such a blatantly spiritual endeavor and for providing the inspiration for the drawings in Chapter 7. We'll always have Napa... :-)

Two people who get their own list are George Pransky and Elsie Spittle. You have been my role models and guides on the path and I am grateful for every minute I get to spend with you. You are to me what I know Syd Banks was to you – loving mentors who, amazingly, I also get to call colleagues and friends.

Next to the bit that will inevitably be as incomplete as it is heartfelt. Thanks to:

♦ Robert Holden for your lovely foreword and years of camaraderie. To know that you even read what I write is humbling; that you like it and find it worthy of mention all the more so.

♦ Paul McKenna for your unwavering support and for over 25 years of friendship.

♦ Everyone who took the time to read early drafts of the book and say kind things about it in public. I know what it is to put your reputation on the line for something, and appreciate your generosity and candor.

♦ The 'hard-core' group of students I mention in the book – my apprentices turned colleagues: Nicola Bird, Maureen Bryant, Ali Campbell, Elese Coit, Stefan Cybichowski, John El-Mokadem, Maggie Gilewicz, Anders Haglund, Libby Hodges, Ana Holmback, Fiona Jacob, Martin Jarnland, Kajen Kanagasabai, Grace Kelly, Sandra Koenig, Dennis Lindsey, Rich Litvin, Bevin Lynch, Toni McGuinness, Donald McNaughton, Susan Motheral, Richard Nugent, Neeta O'Keefe, Barb Patterson, Claire Shutes, Jamie Smart, Jayne Styles, and Sue Trinder. No matter how deep we go, it always feels as if we've only just begun to scratch the surface of what's possible.

◆ All my clients, readers, listeners, and students. We're five books, 10 years of radio, and over 1,000 blog posts into this adventure together – may we continue to have fun and learn heaps for years to come!

And last, but the very opposite of least, thank you to:

◆ My beloved Oliver, Clara, and Maisy, I am soooooo grateful to be your father and so proud of who you are and who you are becoming. The world's not gonna know what hit it…

◆ The love of my life, Nina. You once bought me a mug which said: 'You are the luckiest guy in the world. I would love to be married to me.' I am and I do. You make every cliché about love seem like an understatement. 'You complete me' doesn't even begin to do it justice...

ABOUT THE AUTHOR

David Beeler

Michael Neill is an internationally renowned transformative coach and the best-selling author of *The Inside-Out Revolution, You Can Have What You Want, Supercoach,* and both the *Effortless Success* and *Coaching from the Inside-Out* self-study programs. He has spent more than 25 years as a coach, adviser, friend, mentor, and creative spark plug to celebrities, CEOs, royalty, and people who want to get more out of themselves and their lives. He is also the founder of **Supercoach Academy**, an international school that certifies coaches in the art and science of transformative coaching.

Michael's books have been translated into 16 languages, and his public talks, retreats, and seminars have touched and transformed lives at the United Nations and on six continents around the world. He hosts a weekly talk show on HayHouseRadio.com, and his weekly blogs can be read at MichaelNeill.org and *The Huffington Post*.

His TEDx talk, 'Why Aren't We Awesomer?', has been viewed by over 100,000 people around the world.

You can follow him on Facebook and Twitter:

f   mneill

🐦   @michael_neill

www.MichaelNeill.org

HAY HOUSE

Look within

Join the conversation about latest products,
events, exclusive offers and more.

f Hay House UK

🐦 @HayHouseUK

📷 @hayhouseuk

🖤 healyourlife.com

We'd love to hear from you!